WHAT my FATHER TOLD ME at THREE in the MORNING

MEMORIES OF OUR LIVES, MY ROOTS, GRIEF, DEPRESSION, ANGER AND STRESS SURVIVAL MANAGEMENT

Edward Khiwa, PhD

What My Father Told Me at Three in the Morning
Copyright © 2018 by Edward Khiwa, PhD. All rights reserved.

No part of this publication may be reproduced, stored in a retrieval system or transmitted in any way by any means, electronic, mechanical, photocopy, recording or otherwise without the prior permission of the author except as provided by USA copyright law.

The opinions expressed by the author are not necessarily those of URLink Print and Media.

1603 Capitol Ave., Suite 310 Cheyenne, Wyoming USA 82001
1-888-980-6523 | admin@urlinkpublishing.com

URLink Print and Media is committed to excellence in the publishing industry.

Book design copyright © 2018 by URLink Print and Media. All rights reserved.

Published in the United States of America
ISBN 978-1-64367-034-8 (Paperback)
ISBN 978-1-64367-035-5 (Digital)

Nature
14.09.18

CONTENTS

Preface 5
Forward 7
Acknowledgement 9
Chapter I: The Impact Of World Kingdoms To The Survival And Civilization Of Modern Era 11
Chapter II: The Man's Legacy Of Wisdom To His Son: The Cry Of His Wisdom To The Son 39
Chapter III: Father Reveals Our Heritage The Night Eve Of Departure From Uganda 69
Chapter IV: The Grands & Their Heritages And Tricks For Survival 83
Chapter V: The Orgin Of Dr. Edward Khiwa – Kiwuwa's Grand Parents And Their Line Of Authority 109
Chapter VI: Dr. Khiwa-Kiwuwa Bestowed To Glory And The Presidency Of Over 1-2 Thousands Members Of International Scholars And Phibetadelta 118
Chapter VII: The Day Of The Night Dance 125
Chapter VIII: The Philosophy Of Traditional And Non-Traditional Healers: 131
Chapter IX: My Experience As A Student In Former Soviet Union 133
Chapter X: Interview With My Parents And Sibilings 148
Bibliography 155
Chapter XI: The Birth And Raising Of A First Child In The Newly Married Family 158

Chapter XII: Grand Parents Last Word:
                Their Legacy To Future Generation 174
Summary And Conclusion 187
Assessment Summary Of A Successful Leader And My
Experience As An Administrator..189
Glossary 193
References 195

PREFACE

No historian and gerontologist-aging specialist will use this book in the same manner. Some will use the text as a basis for formal class lectures, supplemented by additional illustration and cases. Others will prefer a less structured approach, using the text as background material for individual and group discussion. Even in medicine, though it is easy to know what honey, wine and hellebore, cattery and surgery, are to know how and to whom and when to apply them so as to affect a cure is no less an undertaking than to be a physician (Aristotle, Nicomachean Ethic, Vol. x).

This book will benefit readers coping and survive against stress, grief, and anger reduction. During the period of down in life, the words of father beeps up: " keep hopes alive, maintain tenacity of triumph and never surrender, keep fighting, will always end up a vector for the world to admire, consult in times of crises; interview with family siblings- pioneers, elderly communities, dialogue with those people with experience in sorrows, anger, grief, stress, and rod scholarly academic experiences from Africa, Europe, and United States, under global universities and colleges. This document is composed of several chapters. Chapter I brings to us, the true measure of man and manhood. Chapter II reveals the father of Dr. Khiwa, Mr. Luyirika, and his philosophy in raising 16 children of boys and girls, men and women and the immigration of his family and his final words of wisdom to those children and citizens of the World. Chapter III focuses at the moment of silence. In this course, here father revealed the sources of his manhood and legacy. Chapter IV brings to the reader the understanding of Luyirikas' grands and his heritage. Chapter V breaks down the history of the great parents of Luyirika's line of origin.

Focuses of his father (Bayise Michael) drafted to fight for the colonial kings in Singapore and Bonea during second World War and his survival from foreign wars and coming back to join his family in Uganda. He came back as a hero of all time in Africa and England. Chapter VI gives attention to the "valley of tears." It reminds the readers where great men and women in the life of Luyirikas have fallen and disappeared from the face of the earth. The tall, the short, black, brown, and all sorts of mankind are laid to rest in the "valley of tears." It is a cemetery where music is kept in the ground to remunerate the history of those who left us. Yes, it qualifies to be called: "The valley of tears. Chapter VII brings "a Night dancer"… for a night to remember by any reader. Night dancers walk at three in the morning, and have magic power to remove the dead from their graves and carry them for their meals. This was one of the occasion when our daddy, and we of our age met this deadly humanity holding a fellow dead human in preparation for the dinner in his home. The details are discussed in this chapter. Chapter VIII focuses on the philosophy, tradition of non-traditional healers in Africa and many parts such as Central America and others that practice "Voodoo," and other abnormal behaviors. Chapter IX gives an experience of my stay in former Soviet Union. The chapter also reveals the heroes of Russia and former Soviet Union and the Great Wonders of the World. Finally, Chapter X focuses on the Round Table conversation between me and my parents. The last time I ever shared a conversation of everlasting experiences with questions and answers. Both, parents are now in the "valley of tears". I never show them again, except in the words of the last message my father and mother left to me to pass to the World.

FORWARD

One of the key characteristics of African society is the ethnic diversity of its population. Although such diversity has greatly enriched our culture, it also has contributed to conflict and social inequality. One way of stratifying a family and its heritage, is by ethnicity and selection. Dr. Edward Kiwuwa's family has several historical social inequality which with fundamental values differs from many Africans. His clan of (Ndiga) is composed of members of ethnic elements due to marriages of various ethnicity. That, such families may never understand the African values since they do not comprehend Africans behaving what they are! For non-African, reading this textbook: "What my Father told me at Three in the Morning," and continue following the events that related to the same cause and history, is a miss-undertaking and lack of understanding the life style of African struggle and habitation to live! The intermarried Caucasian families, have a struggle to fully understand this society and be a part of it! Yet, in Dr. Edward Kiwuwa's clan, there are several of such families. With their children formed between African and non-Africans, together, develop a minority ethnicity within the same clan. Is it a struggle between such families as to where to call the real home for the children; raising them and transform to a true African cultural values! With, Dr. Edward Khiwa-kiwuwa, raised in Africa, but, educated in Diaspora. What cultural values is he to implement in his family abroad! How much of African culture of his, will his children born out of Africa impose upon them? Or they will decide their own, causing a cultural values conflict within a family! When his father was addressing him, the father knew that, his son, would adopt African cultural style of survival, but did not anticipate that, Khiwa-Kiwuwa would end up with two life style backgrounds: African cultural values of origin and Diaspora cultural diversity of the new nation that made his new home.

ACKNOWLEDGEMENT

I am a public librarian in the Metropolitan Library System, Oklahoma. This book is written with travelers and romantics of world who wish to dream and find their roots. Be they from Russia, Uganda, or America, this book gives insight to a passionate man who knows the importance of travel as well as finding one's roots. We deserve to know where we come from, and this book will encourage anyone who reads it to seek out their heritage and family roots. Libraries across the world will treasure this cultured and well thoughtout book of familial love and history. – Randell Baze, Librarian in Metropolitan Library System, Edmond Oklahoma.

CHAPTER I

THE IMPACT OF WORLD KINGDOMS TO THE SURVIVAL AND CIVILIZATION OF MODERN ERA

This chapter relates to cultural competences and its intrinsic value in destroying and or sustaining a nation. It presents how strong kingdoms of the globe, have disappeared due to lack of paying attention to imported foreign culture, and welcoming foreign habits, lifestyles and behavior. Because of these show the oldest South American kingdoms were wiped out and a question is derived that, such ambitious movements how they affected the current kingdoms of our time in Africa, Europe and other parts of the World.

The oldest kingdoms in the world have survived by sharing their authority and power, while held traditions of Kingdoms. The Maya kingdoms, the Incas, of the South America, have all gone with their mighty civilization and prestige. Do the current kingdoms in the world, i.e. the surviving kingdoms of our time in the twenty first century, learn from those kingdoms that no longer exist? What could they do to protect their Kingdoms?

Civilizations of every passing generation have a potential to destroy the surviving kingdoms. Will the 21st internet technology, bring modern culture of civilization that could coordinate the world in one globe; but, what about the prevailing kingdoms of the same century?

How would they protect their subjects from outside influences? Modern Kingdoms such as that in Uganda to survive, they have to be more tolerant while at the same time receiving new ideas and technology from outside world. The modern worlds, and kingdoms, have to accept each other. The civilized communities, and young people, of our time, do not care much about survival of current kingdoms. In summary, its link show the oldest S. American powerful kingdoms which are now ghosts empires. What do current kingdoms and relative subjects learn from such experience! The human society always determines its style of governance. But, with, external influences of internet and foreigners intermingle and intermarry with locals do tend to create a new culture of civic governance causing to weaken and destroy the current kingdoms and civilization.

The old generation of men and women, have a great respect for the kingdoms. Solution would be, to work with young people to cause them to like their kingdoms than destroying them. Baganda, Inca, Aztec; dealing with colonialism: The History of Baganda's Kingdom and Kiwuwa's tribe and his Heritage. One of the sons of the Baganda Kingdom from Buganda Land, in Uganda is focused on in this text, struggling unravel in discovery of his family and the roots of his historical kingdom. Living at Diaspora for many years, he finds challenges upon him to search his home country background and he's determined to learn his blood relationship who died and to meet the remnants of his family and history of their loved ones as well as the African societies and structure. But, he wonders how and where to begin if his family, his father, Luyirika, was nowhere to be found.

THE SON IN HIS JOURNEY TO DISCOVER HIS FATHER AND FAMILY

Luyirika was the father to Edward Khiwa. Khiwa, left his home country to study in foreign lands when he was young and did not know very well his home. In the last days, when he received a visa from the foreign land where he had been educated, he struggled to find his home land after over thirty years. His home Uganda, had plenty of political unrest, and several of his lineage family members had been killed. After securing a visa, the son is now, struggling to discover the roots of his father and siblings.

The trouble is, that, he got the visa from his host country, to go visit his former homeland, while a series of several ruthless unrest political governments was still strong in Uganda, and was unsure of the plight of his former homeland. The young man had been challenged several times of events of life, but the major one, was the greatest news of the death of his senior brother that, he had a bench maker pride for raising him and guiding him in life. It was news he could not bear.

His brother paid much of his education while he was young in early primary and secondary education. Thirty years had now passed by, he had very little contacts with his home country. His parents who were young while he was in Uganda, now had grown old and aged. Yes, the hold up to get a visa, created an opportunity to cause a vacuum in his family. The mails were difficulty to penetrate to the outside world from Uganda. The contacts caused him to be isolated from his family. After several years of struggling alone in foreign lands, his home country gives amnesty to all foreigners that had been in US for so many years. Joy to the World, this young lad, who was now single but with highly academic credentials, is made free to discover his family. The young man is now on the journey to look for his father and the rest of the family and the surviving remnants of his deceased senior brother's family. But, where will he begin, and to pass and whose route and journey to take him to Uganda and meet his loved ones. Fortunately, there was a high school sweet heart, he had left, but he used to send money through friends when he had opportunity to do so. He could not call her, neither would she, but only through family contacts. She kept promising him to marry him when he comes back. Oh, yes, the young man was also in hopes to meet her, on the way to meet his aged family as well the senior brother's family.

THE LOVE ACROSS THE WORLD

Love without money is life without love! While in a foreign lands, this young man had virtually no support from anybody, other than to seek one from the College and part time employment support of his University. He could not get a girlfriend, with hopes that, he could not antagonize his love to his former sweetheart. News constantly came in that she was alive, even after thirty years apart. They had a great commitment of each other, and in early days when communication was clearer, they could call each other on the phone with the little he saved for luncheon. But, as time went on and years past by, one of them was tempted and lost that hung over for him. Men in Uganda could confuse her, that, the man would never come back for you. The days were bad; she had now become a woman. She had to have somebody to buy her perfume, a powder, and a good looking dress. Although she found one, she told him that, her fiancé was abroad but, one day comeback and marry her. The boy while being educated abroad had always a hope to marry his fiancé.

THE DISTANCE IS A CHALLENGE TO LOVE

The young man on achieving his visa, the first thing was now to plan to go back to Uganda, and meet his lover. But, his minds were running up and down all the time. Is she still in love I left her with? Or I am in illusion of love? Keeping commitment for each other is good when you are next to each other, but in a distance, there are many temptations, especially when someone needed something to depend on with her life to sustain. This young man now had grown flamboyant and could challenge disappointments. Before he left Uganda, he had been appointed a responsibility in the Kingdom of his tribe of Baganda. He was always pride of his beginnings that involved to be connected with highly influential families of Baganda Kingdom. But, the period he spent outside Uganda, he was not so sure of the stability of the kingdom he belonged to, and neither after awhile, did he reassured that his girl friend would ever marry her, although, when he arrived in Uganda, the old married woman, left her husband and hid her history of a married woman and came to remind me of her commitment to marry her. She left behind her children and husband, and had put on a teenage lifestyle clothes which could still fit in a marriage life. Yes, I met the challenge. Though I had bought her a gift to keep the promise that long, a quick reminder visited my minds, that HIV was now prevalent, it had to be met with a testing. Of course her husband and children were several miles from my bases of contacts in Uganda. She had been informed that the foreigners had foreign currency. She asked a lot, but, when she refused testing and other issues of life, I became a major concern and had to let it go, but to find out a few days after that she was a married woman with six children. Yes, these would have been my children, had I not decided to leave her and went on to secure education abroad.

DISTANCE LOVE IS A CHALLENGE TO SLEEP

Ever since I flew from Entebbe Airport in Uganda, to study in foreign lands, Juliet stayed in Uganda, but, she went with me in my sleep. I could see her even then, that I was thousands of miles from Uganda. Some days, I could not sleep, but thinking about her. I could feel her charm in dreams. I kept calling her over time with savings I was given for luncheon. Whenever I spread the bed, I could see her throwing a pillow case yet she was not with me. There is nothing more important in life than to love someone in both sleep and dreams. One day, I slept and show her in my hand, to wake up while holding an empty blanket and bed sheets and a towel. What kind of love this was! Love at a distance is not love, but a spiritual or ghost welfare!

Marriage Gambling

Marriage is a secrete institution between a man and a woman and as of lately even people of the same sex. The relationship of the couple varies from home to home. There is no formula for happiness of the couple and their homes. The couples' happiness is more complicated for the foreigners that attempt to have wives and husbands far away from their former lands of origin. Most cases, they may not have enough time to study each other, and to identify each other's way of life, behavior and life style. Some women could agree to marry you to secure opportunity to go to the green pasture abroad. Such opportunities could have never happen if there was no such a stranded man or woman seeking a companion to marry. Many times, the parents of the girls could come forward and introduce their daughter to the boy who leaves abroad, but on adventure in his home to look for a wife. Such adventure journeys are not usually long period in his former country since the vacation given to him from employment in his country of residence is usually between two to one months.

So, you can imagine the cost of a ticket and planning to comeback after another year which most likely would mean the girl introduced to you would be taken by someone else! To avoid such disappointment, a rush arrangement to marry is done and in Uganda, dowry is given to the parents a local traditional marriage.

You may like to go to court for a quick declaration of a vow between each other. But, to the girl who has been looking for opportunity to go abroad, such a vow would mean nothing to her or taken seriously. Sometimes, you may be one of the luck couple and go together abroad after marriage. But, in many cases, she is left home so that you can gravitate a ticket and then follow you when you are back home to say US or England, Australia, etc.

On the other hand, there are foreigners in foreign lands such as US, who want to go home to their former country of origin, but have no visa, or a ticket for doing such deals. Such foreigners are in very complicated conditions. They cannot hold a permanent relationship with a girl friend from their newly adopted new homelands, say in US. Such plan is usually difficulty to succeed.

The girl may have boy friend from their respective high schools. When those boys notice their former girl friend intends to entangle with a foreigner, they will move in quickly to severe that relationship. But, if you play your card cool, sometimes a deal for marriage is done. But, very few relationships of such kinds would last long time. Even if you both fall in love and exchange marriage vows, it does not last for a long time. Marriage of such gambling is a threat to the society and to the family that both of you, tend to bring in the World because of your relationship of each other. The children you both bring in the World tend to suffer consequences for breaking the marriages and divorces are usually imminent.

Keeping vows

With the latest invention of communication technology and internet, couples are easily deceived with a talk of silver tongue from either side. But, to avoid disappointments in marriage is to keep watch at each other and maintain trust of each other, and stay monogamous of each other. If couples submit their love to each other, without reservation, and trust each other in as much as the first love of marriage, God usually protects such marriages for future and many years till elderly. But, the major part is for each couple to learn to give each other a space and stay a distance for a partner to be independent. If you do protectionism, with little or no gifts, and praise of words, such home cannot last. Women want their independence, and yet they also tend to recognize a man who sacrifices for their loves and commitments.

Of course, a home with no children, does not last for most of times. Children tend to act as a chain between couples. But, of all, with a lot of temptations in our neighborhoods, then we must give a thoroughly check of the background of the parents and the loved one background peer friends. Some couples tend to sustain marriages by sharing love among friends of men and women they fully know of each other. But, such relationship could cause disaster since with these latest diseases; trust could spell breaking love with horrible diseases.

This approach should be avoided as much as possible and stay to the true value for love of each other. If one would consider that he or she had the best and beautiful husband and or a best and most beautiful wife in the whole world, such marriage will grow, and disappointments will reduced. Couples that share and give gifts to each other, and control temperament, and take a long time to react when crisis happen in the home, and love, such marriages tend to last as long as both have the same faith, value, and beliefs. The Great Almighty can always provide shelter and assistance of love for each other. Also, those who pray together in whatever form of the couple's faith, such marriages also tend to last long.

This long journey of loving each other is compared to survival of modern kingdoms that have protected their kingdoms, by keeping away imported cultures that penetrate into kingdom subjects and cause bad desires of lives. Outside influences destroy our culture and cause a lack of commitment to each other. How do modern kingdoms of the World, survive and protect their territories; it is also for the husband and a wife not to bring in outside relationship in their marriages. In the discussion that follows, we address the conditions for the survival of modern kingdoms and meeting their respective challenges.

AMERICA'S CHALLENGES IN MARRIAGE AND SOCIETY: FORCING BLACK MEN OUT OF SOCIETY

American society has been besieged with a family and marriage problems, especially in the Black's community. The stability of a nation is the success of the homes and their relative children. No society can be stable if its individual communities are under economic, family and social instability. For instance the research data indicates, that, unravel data, showed that, 1.5 million are missing Black men. The population of black community in America, is about 12% of its national population. If such number of Black men are missing in the homes, it imprints that, more than one in every six black men in the 24 – to -54 age group has disappeared from civic life, mainly because they died young or are locked away in prison. This means that, there are only 83 black men living outside of jail every 100 black women- in striking contrast to the white population, where men and women are about equal in numbers.

SHUT OUT OF SOCIETY

This outstanding shortfall in black men translates into lower marriage rates, more out-of wedlock births, a greater risk of poverty for families and, by extension, less stable communities. The missing men should be a source of concern to political leaders and policy makers everywhere. While the 1.5 million number is startling, it actually understates the severity of the crisis that has befallen African-American since the collapse of the manufacturing and industrial centers, which was quickly followed by the "war on drugs" and mass imprisonment, which drove up the national prison population more than sevenfold beginning in the 1970s.

Federal cases also show higher Rates of public school suspensions for minority students than for white students for identical behavior, suggesting that racial discrimination against black males starts very early in life. The sociologist Devah pager, Havard Professor who has meticulously researched the effect of race on hiring policies, has shown that stereotypes have a powerful effect on job possibilities. In one widely cited study, she sent carefully selected test applicant with equivalent resumes' to apply for low-level jobs with hundreds of employers. MS. Pager found that criminal convictions for black men seeking employment were virtually impossible to overcome in many contexts, partly because convictions reinforced powerful, longstanding stereotypes.

The stigma of criminal record was less damaging for white testers. In fact, those who said that they were just out of prison were as likely to be called back for a second interview as black men who had no criminal history. "Being black in America today is just about the same as having a felony conviction in terms of one's chances of finding a job", she wrote in her book, "Marked : Race, Crime and Finding Work in an Era of Mass Incarceration."

In fact, some studies have indicated that color blind society is not there anymore! Young girls are taught way early, that, turning skin brown, and change texture of the skin to look like population majority of whites, has more chances of securing jobs and more favors in life.

In recent months, the many grievous cases of unarmed black men and boys who were shot dead by the police now routinely captured on video- show how the presumption of criminality, poverty and social isolation threatens lives every day in all corners of American population.

Broken marriages are the products of stranded kids in the streets and increasing poverty in that very society. While black community is moving to change climate, there are still a lot of hurdles to overcome to stay a member society of a great nation, not for a few. The marriages and struggle imbalances is not only left to residents and citizens of foreign born and their relationship to each other, but extends to all walks of society.

THE SURVIVAL OF MODERN KINGDOMS IN COMPARISON TO OTHERS AND CHALLENGES TO THEIR SUBJECTS
LIFE IS A JOURNEY

Traveling in a bus is a journey leading to destination. Life has this course. Some people complete their journey when their lives come to an end, whilst others continue with the bus, on this journey, as to continue with life. Some passengers end lives of this journey with broken hearts, while others end in sleep and untimed moment.

The life of a young man, his father, and his family discussed below, comes from a historical background linked to the phenomenon of kinship of survivors, amended with kingdoms, tribes, civics and a generation composed of civilization of survivors.

The journey discussed above, involves various kingdoms, tribes and other forms of lives. But, in all cases, survival for the fittest, determine how we could hung in the bus to carry on the journey and achieve our mission of life. In many cases, the journey usually ends with popular support and others with natural history of self decay and self destruction. Several World kingdoms have ended that way.

They were eliminated and destroyed by accepting outside influences (imported new civic administrative apparatus, inter-marriages, wars and conquers and others by accepting a status quo of subservient of foreign ideology and compromising principles of survival for the kingdoms and tribes. The kingdoms of South America and other global civilizations that have now extinct, fall back and relaxed as to let in foreign cultures swallowed away their identity.

The Kings and subjects of the kings did little and minimal to protect their identity as such foreign missionaries, partition and fighting for colonies as a source of merchant and economic resources, so did such kingdoms lost their cultural identity, power, civilizations, economic structural wonders, and lost their positions at the global map. For kingdoms and societies mentioned below, are no longer the same and some no longer exist because of compromising principles of their natural identities. Instead of kings and queens to protect their kingdoms, tribes, cultures, they gave in to the outside influences with no limitations available.

That's, the results of extent to compromise principles to a foreign influences, it is the cause of Kings political fall. The Kings had to use their positions to expand their kingdoms and their subjects to protect their boundaries. The Buganda Kingdom has lived over 500 years, due to its governance of hierarchy in totems, clans and aggressive parliament with a prime minister elected by the King. (1)

In Buganda, queens do not lead kingdoms, but advise and cause political stability to the kingdom. Even the times the Kings were taken in exile, due to lack of political accommodation to either colonial leadership or governance at home due to constitutional crisis in government system of Uganda, the subjects of Buganda Kingdom never gave in to their King, a sign of total solidarity in the Kingdom. The elders of the 52 clans never waved on being royal to the leadership of their King, centrally to some of the kings that were discussed below. The young and elders are today keeping the Buganda Kingdom at a frontier, kicking out elements of foreign cultures and political elements.

When the young generations fail to understand the system of cultural kingdom, the elders have to stand strong as it was in 1966 thru 1986 when the Buganda Kingdom was restored in Uganda. But, for such a period, many elderly were now dying off, and if the period was to continue, a generation of subjects who did not know

King, would have grown, and it would have been steady growth of declining of the Kingdom of Buganda.

It is the elderly and young and position of influence from the King that is creating a balance to keep the Buganda Kingdom a float, and an admirable Kingdom of all in the World. The Baganda Kingdom has been the Center of civilization for the Uganda's population. If the Baganda, continue with this position, it will be a formidable kingdom in East African region since the growth of population of Uganda and other African community is a fast pace in the region.

Protecting the Kingdom of Buganda Kingdom in Uganda's mentioned in earlier discussion, colonial administrators in foreign lands had much to do with destruction of the indignity culture of the nationals they met in their countries. The standards of culture vary from country to another. Who determines that one's culture is better than another and how do you judge it. It is the foreigners that create a system to introduce their own identity. Where the locals resisted, the foreigner administrators, called the nationals, savages. Sir Winston Churchill, called several groups of Southern Sudan, the Madi –Sudans, and the in habitants in high lads of Kenya as sages since they could not wear clothes of the English speaking community, speak English language of the advanced human and so he degraded the nationals to the level of savages, which led to set up a policy of the native Indians and local Africans not to hold lands in high lands of Kenya. That, they could not see savages share their own neighborhoods. That, high lands were saved for high civilized society of English people.

The comparison of English, French and Arabs in exploration of new world.

English exploration & geographical society: Their major mission was conquest of foreign lands for to settle, reward themselves the resources of the natives, and create a life of the sphere of influence in the sun. They made earned effort to rule under the kings and their subjects where ever there were kings and to create a level of comfort for the natives to feel that they were benefiting from the colonial masters. For instances, kings of Bunyoro such as Kabalega had to be forced to lose power and authority of the kingdom of his subjects for refusing to welcome the colonial subjects. On the otherhand, Buganda Kingdom welcomed the foreigners as such the English colonial introduced a system of indirect rule. That way, the English ruled under the leadership of Baganda king. The Baganda king and their subjects were more sensitive that, they had crafted advanced civic institutions of public administration that lined up well to that of the queen and kings of England. This included court system, local administration, communication levels of authority and land management which was more exclusively owned by the King of Buganda.

English language introduced in colonial territories vs Luganda language

The English colonial policy of indirect rule and civic organization was to keep English in control, but with influences of the natives. The English language was taught and introduced as a language for the elite. The Baganda resisted it. Even if the Baganda kingdom had welcomed the English and extended a friendly language taught in earlier years of native schools in Uganda. The British language, to avoid defiance, introduced the English language to advanced institutions. The English language was introduced instead, as an elite language ie. For those natives who had older ages and education so that the British would use the specialists in English language to be spokesmen for the colonials to the masses of natives. This way, indirect rule would survive. In addition, they made education system expensive in lower education system and schools but, it would be free to the entrants to the University. This created educational system a prestigious institution more for the elites; since only English speaking people would enjoy benefits and would be considered civilized. By the way, if they had introduced Luganda at early ages of education, it would have wiped out, the Luganda speaking community and the Buganda kingdom would have disappeared. This method, the Baganda was smart to protect their kingdom.

The French system of influence

The French policy, was to educate the masses. It was the opposite to that of English system. The French language was taught to the young people, on the village level and communities. You would notice Franc language spoken by the natives at a low level. The French provided education to all natives. That, made it easier to introduce French Language in all areas of the French peaking community. The French educational system gave opportunity for masses to be educated. This way, in comparison with British system, the French provided a system with no strong intentions for home influences to govern the natives. By speaking the language, the natives could understand each other better than for English system that was all in needs of an interpreter. The governors were used to extend the British influences in the colonial lands. On the same note, the kingdoms that admitted French to be readily spoken at all levels, did not survive and have strong kingdom.

The legacy of Arab- East African Trade

The Arabs used to trade south wards on the Monsoon winds. They travelled to the costs of East Africa, with coastal landings in Mombasa and Biscayne harbors. They were the first foreigners to come to the coastal lands of east Africa. In contrast, though slavery was also practiced as it was the same with European colonialists, they had no motives of dominating natural resources for the natives. Their mission in the trading practice of East Africa, was to extend the Islamic culture of influence. There was on several occasions when they intended to expand inside the continent, but they met fierce resistance from natives ie. the Kikuyu worriers and other strong tribes in east Africa that would not allow their slavery system continue and survive in the continent of the region of East Africa. They did not open administrative territories, but left a legacy of the Moslem religion and a legacy of mixed words of African languages and Arabs words, forming Swahili languages. Their influence was not much felt like that of western colonials in opening colonies and controlling them. But, the Swahili language is becoming relatively accepted as a medium method of communication in Africa, but with a tough resistance from the Kingdoms of Uganda. The kingdom subjects seem to fear that their culture ie. Luganda would be dominated and virtually disappear, causing the extermination of the Kingdoms. The Baganda, Banyoro and other tribal kingdoms, have survived by protecting their local languages and keeping boundaries of the foreigners and their influences. On virtually, the Arabs' greatest legacy to the Kingdom of Buganda, was the white attire well known for the Major in marriages for the introduction ceremonials dowry of bride and bridegroom as is readily observed at the cover page of this document when my wife invited me to her parents of which I and my family worn for the special occasion. It was a special occasion where my eldest brothers and Sisters had to join in me in visit to my wife's family to deliver to them gifts and gratuities for good raising of their daughter.

Culture and Global Village of oneness

The modern technology of the 20th and 21st Century, and the creation of the internet and modern travel in short period from one country to another, has caused a challenge to the conservatives as to how long they can hold on their culture, language and kingdoms.

The sphere of influences will soon disappear in many kingdoms due to the association with foreigners and their imported culture in the midst of their civilization. The historical powerful kingdoms of the World, are slowly gone and forgotten. The British Kingdom is slowly vanishing since it accepted to receive cultures from foreigners that were more of their former colonialists. The English language is a legacy of powerful English speaking community. Today, we can forget the English colonialists, but, we cannot forget that English language is a unifying front to many countries around the world. The powerful English kingdoms, the Swedish, the Denis, and many others, are slowly disappearing. Ultimately, the English speaking community will be left with the Russian speaking community whose king, ie. Elisabeth era disappeared from the face of the earth with the Soviet

Union revolution under its leaders, the Lenin, Stalin, Gorbachev and others. Today, the queen of England is a figure head, and yet, in the centuries ago, the kingdoms were the most centers of lives in the English system. If the king had not accepted a version of new role she has for the kingdom, it would have been much weaker than it is today, and even today, a more aggressive protection of the kingdom is eminent if the survival of it will continue for future centuries.

Kingdoms Resistance to Change OR sign of Unity for Progress of a society

In some circles, there are arguments for pros and cons for hereditary rulers. Are hereditary rulers a disservice to democracy and development or it provides a climate of stability of a society. In history of mankind, there have been such both arguments. In the recent survey of 700 college students and citizens of nations that have and without kingdoms, there were mixed results from both young people. In summary, democracy and development is an argument of debate. Human civilization has revealed that, wherever there was a king in that region, there was significant progress. Reviewing historical progress that exist in emerging areas, where there are no kingdoms, the argument would be that, it would have come at certain time, except that the prevailing society would not be patient with the kingdom policies in those areas with no kingdoms. There has been more stability in regions with kings than without kings. Kings have traditionally demanded orders of their subjects. Developments of unequal level were observed during or when kings were in power. Observation of the Pyramids of Egypt, under the Pharos, It is one of the wonders of the World. The Byzantine, Abyssinia, and construction of the palaces with mighty hands of kings subjects of Buganda, setting up the glory of Kasubi, (Grass huts for burial grounds of kings in Buganda Kingdom and was recently declared by the society of World scientific community as a glory to the World) one other wonders of the World. The kings and queens cool off temperature of political pressure from masses towards the society be regulated as we move in the 21st century and beyond. The kings and kings' subjects have been left behind in the penetration of foreign cultures into their kingdoms. The religious powers of kingdoms have been tamed for the wave of change from Regulation of Kingdoms. The powers and authorities of hereditary rulers needs to foreign contacts due to internet and immigration of each other's nation. No one country can afford to be an island. Religious services from religious leaders under the kings need to be governed with changes in the national constitution, but leaving the laws of religions untouched. However, extreme laws that would temper with people's and subjects lives ie. cutting people's throats during services for not obeying service rituals, or on orders of the King, should not be allowed to continue in the modern century. There by the power of the king should be eliminated for he or she fails to protect the lives of his /her subjects. The kingdom to make a difference to its society, it should be governed under a federal system of governance. Each region in the country should provide care for its residents in that kingdom or region. As powers and authorities hereditary authorities will be regulated, the constituencies that seek to protect the culture and glory of the Kingdom will be reduced.

Reduction of Sickle cell diseases

Sickle cell is one of the hereditary diseases that individuals exposed to or carry due to the choices of the parents. It mostly originates due to blood cross bleeding. With inter marriages, of cousins and have children from loved ones of the same family to which parents are of the same origin, the blood pass over from one source of the parent to that of the child. Hopefully that, one parent may carry it from the same respective parent to cause what we call a carrier. It is a painful experience for children with blood sickle cell. Their life expectancy is really beyond twenty to forty years. Sickle Cell diseases are more prevalent in areas where slave trade was practiced such as in African American of US and countries around Mediterranean Sea where slave trade was carried on for a long time. It is also prevalent in ethnic cousins, and blood to blood intermarriages. (2)

The Kings Role and Kingdom In Uganda

The eleven million people of Buganda kingdom are ruled under their king who oversees their lines and totem of birth.

Dr. Edward Khiwa, the grandparent and the leader of the totem, he is now addressing his subjects in his role as a leader of the totem and is now assigning names of the babies that has been brought to him in his clan.

Names in Buganda kingdom are assigned by the line of your birth to avoid conflicts and cross marriages. Each line is governed by the hereditary administrator whose leadership is for life and is passed on to his successor. It cannot be changed and it leaves for life. Each totem leader has a ritual of managing the king's subjects on behalf of the King. Even if the political climate dissolves the kingdom, the totem leaders were set up to carry on in the absence of the King. The king and totem leader have a responsibility to carry on the tradition of the ancestors and memories of those that left the current generation. This kind of belief is very strong in Uganda and that's one of the causes for people in Uganda to like their king. He is the chair of the fifty (50) totems which have been carried out for centuries beyond. When a child is born, the totem leader assigns the names to protect infringing to the other totems. Overall, no totem leader gives a name to new birth unless that birth belongs to his totem and is responsible to its success in life and traditional guidance. This practice has saved the kingdom troubles of the famine, diseases and protection against sickle cell diseases.

The King is loved by subjects when he acts as a king, provides leadership and demands honor and glory to protect the history of the culture. As long as the subjects like the king, so the kingdom will never disappear like that of the Mayo Kingdom. That kingdom, used to be more powerful than the regular governments of our time. However, when it did not protect the kingdom, and allowed foreigners to dominate their religions and cultures, it increased perils to the society and kingdom and it eventually vanished from the face of the earth and many more are following the same trend. We should put in place regulations that protect the subjects from being exploited and also protect the king and his kingdom.

Baganda tribe (Uganda) being the largest, with a Kingdom that has survived between five and one thousand years, will regain its international power and influence. This was not afore seen by other cultural kingdoms of the World such as those of Incas; Mayo's whose civilization and culture no longer in existence.

THE HUNTING OF WHITE ANTS AT THREE IN THE MORNING IN THE VILLAGES OF UGANDA (AFRICA)

Growing up with your father, have fun together, and sharing a lot of life experiences, makes adulthood life of that child the most memories of everlasting. I got to know my father real well. We moved together several times in the villages of Uganda during the days and nights. During the days, we did activities related to life such as playing games, going to church, work together in farms and fields of cotton, picking coffee, and eat together. At night, we used to travel distances to beat the opening time of the trading market for the sales of our farms. Late in the night when everyone was asleep, me and my father joined the activity ritual of the residents of our local village. At three in the morning everyone would wake up and head towards the anti-hill to collect white ants. This ritual is carried out by the residents of that village using a mantel of light from burning wood. Much of these activities had to be conducted at three in the morning for that was the time when the white ants would be free from their queen mother in the anti-hill. Preparation for that site is done ahead during the day. A circumference of hole of about two inches is dug and all debris is cleared from it. It is said that, only the active that could sacrifice their sleep of such late in the morning could catch the white ants. If one wakes up late, he could meet all white ants raised and flown. White ants hunting are a fun game to participate in at the village level. It is fun to notice fellow village mates, waking up at the same time at such a late hour and holding light mantel of firewood, and holding it up to see at a distance. Deep in villages, apart from the cities, there was virtually no electricity that provided power for the village people to enjoy. But, the village residents had to improvise themselves with whatever they could find to survive.

Usages of white ants as a game

White ants play several rolls in the village life. They are for example: 1). A source of vegetable to the families in villages; 2). It is a source of medicine; 3). It is a source of income to the village people who barely have a strong source of income, and finally, it is used as an appetizer and food recreation cuisine before a major dinner of the family. If it is well cared for, the amount collected is used to pay school fees for the children.| (4) Yes, of course, this was unordinary family that lived in a simple home, and always had shared dinners together with the family. | (5)

An African home at night, is characterized by the prestige of the fathers' leadership of the home in the family. To protect his wife and children, against beasts, scavengers, and boyfriends of his daughters; daddy had to be strong and vicious to uninvited home guests. Boys at the village, tended to move in girls parents homes in a quiet manner, before the parents came to know about it, their daughters had been made pregnant and had missed schools and a future career. Father had to be protective of his daughters and also to guard his home against these nasty village boys.

African home at night, especially when the moon is at its brightest, the daughters were not allowed to date, only to go to schools.

Hunting white ants at night, is a game of great ritual in the African village of Uganda….. only men can wake up at that morning hour of three in the morning, and challenge the bush of anti hill to fetch stranded white ants with their queen mother.

It is a great honor from the fellow village residents, each running after his game site and location. Constant consultation is done to assist in hunting a big game of white ants. Early morning plans, are done during the day, in preparation of the forthcoming game at three in the morning (the white ants).

Significance of white ants to an African home in Uganda.

During the day, usually the fetched white ants from the bush, a night before, is steamed in a saucepan and spread on a mat for the sun to strike directly at the steamed white ants. Protecting the site of the ant-hill is not a simple matter. Always, your neighbors will strive to marginalize the cause of your big success and so would make effort to take that site away from you.

My father was always alert to such potential enemies and intruders. Apart from losing the sleep of that late in the morning, my father and his fellow residents in the village, had to take precautions of the beasts in the forests and reptiles. It was important to safeguard your territory with proper tools.

One day, we had a major challenge when a leopard walked lose at that late hour and came to visit our anthill where we were hunting our game. My father had made a point to me, — "never walk at night without a safeguard of your life"." You never know which surprising enemy would strike first, and or where she could be hiding.

Daddy always made effort to move with the following weaponry: (1) a spear and (2) a club of big stick and (3) a big knife. He always insisted that, a man should always show leadership, courage and stamina with vibrant while facing unknown beasts and other challenges of life.

The Day of test of a man and a parenthood of a father: It was that day and that silent late night hour!

During that night, we were, me and my father, virtually the only hunters in that neighborhood for the next neighbor was about two blocks away from where we were that night. During that late night at three in the morning, a beast charged at our game site and hid in the bush. It snoozed! When, the beast rolled its screaming, I became so much frightened that I ran behind the back of my father who was by this time getting ready to encounter with this uninvited beast. A leopard is a vicious animal when is hungry and strikes first unless you know how fight back.

Of course, we had no help from our village mates. We were on our own alone! A leopard moves in tricks and in disguised circles against its pray, so that, it is difficult to target it for a full fight. It depends on its smell to identify its enemies, and other foes.

It was a blizzard moment for me, as a child. I could see myself trembling, urinating in pant, as if I had been told. I new all my future including my potential future teenage girlfriend in the village, entirely depended on skills of my father.

But, my father who was at this time armed with his spear and a big club had got ready to undergo frontier with this fierce animal.

It was terrific a wild and scaring animal that commanded a respect from other fellow beasts in the jungle.

My father, commanded, — "Kiwuwa", as it was my name;" you are now a man". It's your turn to survive this beast or to go with it, he exclaimed!

As he got his fighting artilleries, and strong hold of his position, he also told me that, now the war for the survival of the best had began. He asked to look after myself at that hour. But, I have no weapon, I charged, Daddy! You should always walk armed yourself and know how protect from danger. There was no much time to discuss the rest. It was now a critical hour. His final words before he went quietly to act was:" Be in charge of other residents at home and in the village if we survive this one".

WHAT MY FATHER TOLD ME AT THREE IN THE MORNING

A leopard had a wild sharp deep noise that night, which affected the village. Several people who had heard the screaming of the leopard, anticipated danger at the position we were both, me and my daddy, stationed in relative to the beast and they were now coming to our rescue! But, they had no weapons, guns etc, other than stones and sticks. The night was a confusing. It was dim, dark in some areas and bright in others. The moon was besieged. They came anyway….. coming where? everyone was scared and could hardly organize any mutiny against this beast, since they were more nervous than we, who were at the front line.

It was not easy. They could have gone back to sleep. The beast was hungry and was ready to charge! So, was my father! My job at that tense of moment, was to hung on his dear protruded clothe for protection!

My father had been raised by my grandfather. My grandfather had fought in colonial wars of 1945's, so, had been charged to train his son to be a survivor by fighting with all available tools at times of danger.

As people were now moving around our position of the anti hill, my father had been holding firm in his hand a big club and a big knife. The more the leopard made a wild noise, it involved other animals and the nearest of all was the king of the jungle, the lion.

I did not know by this time that my father had now thrown a spear to the leopard and it was by then fainting. Now, when other fellow village residents joined in, they heard a lot of skills that scared off the lion to charge in a different direction.

It was looking for either one of the village residents but, my father had already kept the leopard under his control.

The lion went in a different direction since it missed the target of the leopard but instead went for another play which we noticed was a few distance away.

Meantime, the village residents joined in to give a hug to my daddy and a last blow to the dying leopard.

Shortly, my father told me and the residents that had come to our rescue that: "Beasts are scared as you are, but, they will easily detect the weakness of their target from fainting."

Father said, to me, that," when one day you have a family you need to use these techniques to protect the family and personal life". But above all, he said," leadership is crucial to survive in this world and stamina, courage is imminent, especially as you fight off intruders off your lives, "He ended. I replied that, what has gone with me to night, and watching you, I had to a training exercise of leadership to all and before mankind, a lesson of my life time! I am ready to command leadership leading to human survival and you have just proved by teaching me one! Thank you Daddy!! I cried with a hug to him and so did others. To be brave you start young and challenge the World. He concluded with aloud voice.

FOUR LIFE FACTORS & AGES 1 THRU 10

The author here states, that life has four factors that has built strengths for the author to write this document. The pillars that have supported the author: 1). the sources of security2). The sources of power, 3). The sources of Wisdom and the sources of 4). Adoptability. For one to understand life survival, must determine: 1) the source of security for that allows him to be obedient and civic understanding.

This young man when he was in various nations around the World, he respected laws and civic governance. Similarly, the Kingdoms to survival and return to their glories, must work with the Federal System of governance. Understanding the sources of power is an important cultural element.

The relationship between the national government and the Kingdom is important as to how power is shared. It works smooth when power is shared in national fraction of federal system of governance. An individual has to accept the hierarchy of leadership for him to survive. The Kingdoms that lost their kingdoms ignored their history and lack of understanding power and authority. The Wisdom is a factor built within us based to our earlier experience in early years. The researchers in the studies of psychology state that, wisdom is developed in early years, between one (1) and ten (10).

The experience a child masters in those early years i.e. Learnt from parents, siblings, and peers develop the child's ability for a wisdom. The author developed ability to survive and communicate to outside world due to his early years of life; and finally the adaptability is an important element to go along well with everyone in the domain of the influence both outside and inside influences. When a subject is capable to adopt and easily adjust, he/ she can have few challenges to survive on his or her own. This factor is what makes us different from other people.

When the author was in European countries, he had never been in homes with Europeans and other forms of people of walks of lives. But, because, his parents prepared him for challenges of adoptability, he managed to do well abroad. For example, one day one of his friends asked him, "When you were in Uganda, did you ever looked at the mirror and identify the color of your skin?" He replied that, in his early days in Uganda, he did not even know about human color and skin.

He mentioned that, he did not even know poverty. "What is poverty?" (3) There was no poverty in his early years of life. There is poverty when you compare your life achievements with another ones' leverage. But, in the elementary school ... Katikamu, an earliest school of humble beginning of the author, there was no one to compare with. All of students in that school had no shoes, had no cars, and had virtually had to walk to school. There was luncheon prepared at school but, left over's was the luncheon for majority of the students that walk to school several miles from their homes.

Whenever it rained there were no umbrellas, only to use bananas leaves. So, you can notice that, poverty exist if other people have more than what you have. Otherwise, you are all happy and enjoy lives equally as it was with this author. But, the author also states, that, when he left the village life, challenges of haves and have not also came in. To that, he attributes his joy to his elder siblings, Joshua Kigeya, who gave him his first pair of shoes to wear it while going to secondary school. Life changed gradually when he was admitted to study in a secondary school with children from the wealth families. The continued readings lead you to the picture of the author and his earliest classmates.

THE TRUE MEASURE OF A MAN- THE LUYIRIKAS FAMILY AT KATIKAMU & WOBULENZI, BUGANDA

The true measure of a man is to be able to provide for both his children and his family. Luyirika the father of the author did exactly what is said above. Kiwuwa was one of the sons of Erisa Luyirika. Luyirika was relatively famous in Adventist community; here would be regard as cycles of influence.

The Luyirikas, i.e. Kiwuwa and his siblings were raised by both their parents in the remote areas of Buganda. The parents of Luyirika were famous in the kingdom of Buganda. They educated him at Mityana where his humble beginnings started. When he responded to a call of the missionaries from abroad, the organized church of missionaries sent him away from his family circles to deter him from going back to a belief different than the religions of the missionaries. He raised some of his children in remote areas of the Buganda Kingdom, while others were reared when he was transferred to a distance from the Capital of Uganda. The father of Luyirika was a veteran of World War II that was one of the survivors of the First World War that had been sent to fight other countries on behalf of the British colonial masters in Uganda.

He established that, the children (Luyirika and his siblings had to go to school and supported it. Luyirika was well educated in all areas of academics that included, mathematics, English and literature and other African languages.

Luyirika and his father used to venture local brewery to the king's palace. Luyirika did a great job to educate his children.

Baganda (bägän'də) also called Ganda, the largest ethnic group in Uganda. Bagandas comprise about 17% of the population and have the country's highest standard of living and literacy rate. Their traditional homeland is Buganda, an area of central and southern Uganda. (4)

The Ganda came into contact with the British in the nineteenth century, resulting in widespread social upheavals in Buganda. The population of the Ganda, said to have numbered three million during the reign of Muteesa I (1856–1884), diminished to around a 1.5 million as a result of famine and civil war.

By the early 1900s, their population had been reduced to around one million as a result of an epidemic of sleeping sickness. Changes to Bugandan society, the first major change being the introduction of a standing army during Muteesa I's reign, were accelerated when Buganda became the centre of the newly formed Uganda Protectorate as part of the British Empire in 1894. Land which had previously belonged solely to the *Kabaka* was divided among the *Kabaka* and the tribal chiefs. Many of the old clan burial-grounds, previously considered sacred, were desecrated.

The Inca civilization (or Inka) began as a tribe in the Cuzco area, where the legendary first Sapa Inca, Manco Capac, founded the Kingdom of Cuzco around 1200. Under the leadership of the descendants of Manco Capac, the Inca state grew to absorb other Andean communities. In 1442, the Incas began a far-reaching expansion under the command of Pachacutec. He founded the Inca Empire or Tahuantinsuyo, which became the largest empire in pre-Columbian America.

The spread of colonial empires was reduced in the late 18th and early 19th centuries by the American Revolutionary War and the Latin American wars of independence. However, many new colonies were established after this time, including for the German colonial empire and Belgian colonial empire. In the late 19th century, many European powers were involved in the Scramble for Africa.

The population of African and Eurasian peoples in the Americas grew steadily, while the number of the indigenous people plummeted. Eurasian diseases such as smallpox, influenza, bubonic plague and pneumonic plagues devastated the Native Americans who did not have immunity. Conflict and outright warfare with European newcomers and other American tribes reduced populations and disrupted traditional society. The extent and causes of the decline has long been a subject of academic debate, along with its possible characterization as genocide.

Nearly all scholars now believe that widespread epidemic disease, to which the natives had no prior exposure or resistance, was the overwhelming cause of the massive population decline of the Native Americans. They reject both of the earliest European immigrants' explanations for the population decline of the American natives. The first explanation was the brutal practices of the Spanish conquistadores, as recorded by the Spanish themselves. This was applied through the encomienda which was a system to protect warring tribes as well as to teach the natives the essence of the Spanish language and the Catholic religion. Probably the main reason Africans, rather than Native Americans, became slaves in America was that Africans and Europeans shared immunities to Old World diseases. (5)

REVIEW QUESTIONS

1. What role do foreigners play as they settle in a new world?
2. Is life a journey or a destiny with a cause?
3. What are the true measures of a human being?
4. What should be the best legacy of a father to his family and children?
5. Discuss and give reasons," when human beings are still alive, we give them little value to what they are, but when they pass away, we start to look at them and their contributions."
6. What in your mind are the four life factors that make a human being?
7. Should man be friendly to beasts and wild animals?
8. Should money be a factor in choosing a career?
9. What is the relationship between colonialism and Imperialism, and how has it affected emerging nations
10. What is the comparison between Arab traders of East Africa and slave trade triangle of Western Africa and their counter allies of Western Europe?
11. How can we raise sons and daughters who are heroes and patriotic? What is the effect of single parents to developing a heroic generation?

CHAPTER II

THE MAN'S LEGACY OF WISDOM TO HIS SON: THE CRY OF HIS WISDOM TO THE SON

D*ifficulties arise in times like this, to write a memorabilia about one of the few legends in the history of the 20th century. As we fold back the end of the century and cherish the 21st period,* our minds and hearts from time to time recognize those personalities that have made history an annals and epochs in extending our civilization, and paved it through others as a lineage for many generations to come.

The author of " What my father told me at Three (3) in the Morning." Dr. Edward Khiwa- Kiwuwa in Grade one and his friend, Wamala in the same grade, who goes to Kalere Church in Uganda. front right is: Kiwuwa, Khiwa. (Photo provided by friend)

EDWARD KHIWA, PHD

THE MAN ERISHA LUYIRIKA & HIS ELDER BROTHER JONATHAN MUSOKE WALUNG'AMA FORMER RESIDENTS OF (MITYANA- NAMAKOFU, UGANDA)

> *Few people ever knew who the man by the above names was, and as yet others who had the opportunity to study and understand the man did ignore and never cared. The history of the man has come but his contributions are yet to be felt by more millions yet to come. His legacy is an attribute through those he apprehended to protect the legacy of his history.*

The history of man is the eminent of his philosophy and principles. The success and protection of our civilization has held high to the standards of the few individuals who never compromised their beliefs and values. Such a man was Erisha Luyirika. Contribution to the frame work of human well being is a challenge to all humanity, but recognizing the contributors is a credit difficult to forego by others. Luyirika was a citizen to one of the nations of Africa. Due to difficulties of achieving publications and recording for fore father's deeds in Africa's nations, more so in Uganda the nation of Luyirika's birth, are a lot of wisdom, knowledge, training, and skills that are usually lost that would have been an inventory for future reference had it been that they had been written and recorded from people such as him.

By the time we turn to recognize them, such legends have by then left our time for ever. It is of paramount that, his offspring, grandees and those yet to come and the loved ones of his ancestry should carefully uphold the banners of the beliefs and principles and philosophy the humanity would call a legend. Luyirika understood his beliefs of Adventists and represented his parents' family as a leading pioneer of a movement in the missionaries to the churches originating from countries other than his own. It was an act of stout sacrifices that during his time there were hardly Christian believers who understood what the philosophy of Adventists movement was all about. He was born at the beginning of the twentieth century. His birth day of 1906 was preceded by international wars which involved many citizens of nations around the world and some from his home Uganda in which it were involved. His parents' records of achievements were difficulty to recognize as printing press and record keeping management was virtually none. We hardly have a record of his parental achievements.

LUYIRIKA'S LIFE AS A TEENAGER

Luyirika was born to a family of the most dominant tribes in Uganda, "The Baganda tribe". The Baganda people are proud of their tribe. Their tribe is composed of 52 clans and each one is managed by a Sweden is the most hospitable country amongst the 25 coutries I have stayed and worked with, next of course to Uganda, and US. I certainly enjoyed Swedish language and the Swedish people. Stockholm is an international City where everyone enjoys to stay. Foreigners come from around the World, especially inSoutnern Europe. This picture shows my life in Uganda after high school. The author of "What My father Told me at Three in the Morning, and the Days of our lives."

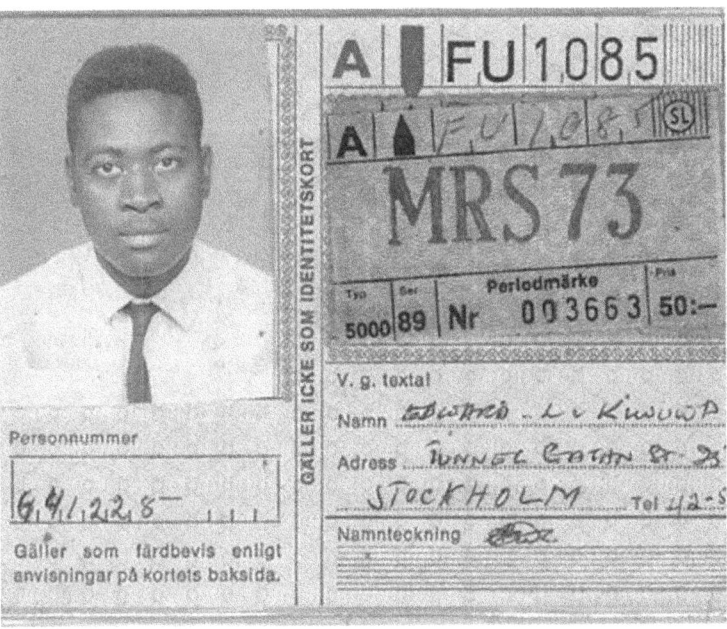

Dr. Edward Kiwuwa- Khiwa, in Uganda
(Photo provided by former college peer)

Photo credit by author.
Here, in the pictures above standing with my old friend when we were fainting with cold blizzard weather in that giant nation of Soviet Union or Russia as of today.
Dr. Edward Kiwuwa- Khiwa, in Russia

My experience of Russian as a country and People as a student.

In September 1971, we arrived to go to the Soviet Union on the scholarship. It was my first time to travel to Russia, which was at that time, the Soviet Union. We were promised that the language of instruction for our courses was to be in English language. At least, that is what the Soviet Union ambassador in Uganda told us on farewell dinner to his country. We were a few of us, but we did not know each other. The scholarships to which I had one, were earmarked for both academic and friendship generated by the Soviet Union government to boost friendship with third world countries. Of course, at those days, Uganda had a great friendship with this great giant Russian-Soviet nation. President Obote of Uganda at that time, had mobilized the Citizens of Uganda to move to the left of friendship with Soviet Union. By the time of our departure, the country had been converted to another presidential leadership of Field Marshall, IDD Amin. But, then, it was getting tough to exercise freedom and career professionalism. Those were tough days in Uganda. The coup took a lot of people's lives in Uganda. Since President Obote, had abolished the loving kingdoms in Uganda, in particular that of Buganda which is still the largest and with highest density. At the takeover of IDD Amin, I could see with my naked eyes, people losing their properties, housing, etc for being sympathizers to Obote's regime that had eliminated the Kingdoms in Uganda especially that of Kabaka (king) of Buganda. Several buildings were burnt. A lot of peoples' animals and their food plantations were cut in pieces, burnt and destroyed. Hunger returned to the country since a lot of people had nothing to eat. In other side, people that lost their properties were killed, burnt with petrol and others cut with big knives for being supporters of the hated government led by president Obote. The surviving victims had to run to neighboring countries, and others to hide in further down thick forestry to avoid being killed. While in the forest, some of them, were killed by wild animals, and others killed themselves.

Yes, the people of Uganda, especially the (Baganda of Buganda kingdom) love their king as a mother loves her baby. Obote was hated mostly because, he destroyed the Kingdoms, and also his policies that, likened the youths to move towards socialist –Marxist ideology. The parents did not like that, but, since the government had money, they had to comply unwillingly to please the President. And those who participated in the behaviors that led to the destruction of the King of Baganda, had to face a ravage of King loving subjects. While in exile, in England, the death of the King of Baganda, Sir Edward Mutesa, affected the entire nation and increased more hatred for Obote himself and his regime had been toppled. People in Buganda a population of about 37% of the people of Uganda, had to wear back clothe as a sign of the loss of their King. Sir Edward Mutesa his death in England, was controversial. Since no one closely observed the last act of his death, there were a lot of speculations of the cause of his death. It included, poison and other activities not provable. Since the English government did not lock up anybody in the prison, the death remained what it is today. The King, Sir Edward Mutesa, had to pass on his son, by the names "Mutebi, Walugembe" to take over the throne. He is now, the King of Baganda, and his office is in

Bulange (Kampala, the capital of Uganda), the headquarters of his kingdom.

Certainly, the take over and bring in a new president, and the environment as it was, acquiring a scholarship from abroad regardless the country it came from and the culture it had. When the opportunity showed up, I jumped on it and accepted the offer and travelled for scholarship in Soviet Union.

As I mentioned earlier that, even if I had been in other countries before, the Soviet Russia was a challenge. We left at 3:00 P.M from Entebbe (International airport of Uganda), with soviet Russian Aeroflot. It was a big airliner. It was equal to DC- 10. It had stories, up and down. We were treated like in Uganda while in the plane. We had English language used at the plane and the food served was very familiar at home in Uganda.

It was a swift plane, some tumbles here and there. Finally, we reached Moscow airport in the next morning. We were welcomed by several junior high school girls, who had rose flower and with sweet words" Welcome to our Country." We were shortly lifted into several buses that were waiting for us. We ended up in a hotel, since all affairs of immigration had between settled by the hosting government.

We were then, given several University students that were studying English language to guide us. I protested that, we were told English language was the language to be used. But, the students' guide affirmed us that Russia or Soviet Union did not recognize English as a national language for the soviet people. Instructions at the Universities, cafeteria, museum, theaters, and other public institutions, must use Russian language. I asked to go back to Uganda, but the student guide was advised to inform me that, the government had spent a lot of Rubbles to bring me to Moscow that, it was of no use to talk or think about it! So, I had to stand and get used to new life as a married woman make effort to know her husband's after marriage.

After three days, in the hotel, they came in our chambers and had brought buses that took us to buy clothes from the "Big shopping Stores," like that of Super Wal-Mart. We were all the time accompanied by our faculty who knew nothing about English language. We had to learn how to communicate to them in Russian language. We used sign language for everything ie. "Milk" we called it "marako." It was fun to learn that new language with those guides and the public at large.

They bought for us, warm clothes. They made sure we knew how to wear them. They told us:" Russia and Soviet Union is a called country, and Moscow the capital is much colder." We were told, if the security highway patrol would find you on the way, in winter as such without wearing your nine (9) pieces, you would not only get a ticket while walking, but you would as well be picked up and go to jail. The orientation was clear, that, waking up on time, and putting on the nine piece on our bodies was the major part of our orientation. We were also notified, that," Shapka head Hair hat" or Russian call it "Cwanka" and a warm jacket and shoes etc. were crucial. It was also noted that, going by electric bus, and under- train were very much necessary for us to survive in Russian country.

As you see above, I have put on and my friend from the same country. He was coming from Luwero district in Uganda. We met together at this juncture on our way to buy winter clothes. It was fun to be in Russia, because one day, they showed us the burial ground of Lenin. By those day, his body was embalmed and was left to the surface for the public to view him as a tourist. He was dead, but had exchange of guards every an hour. We had to line up a mile to view his body. People in Russia tend to respect him as someone very important. Of course, we toured the coldest place on the earth, the "Yakut" a town found in the far north of Russian Republic. It is so called that, the government used it in the underground of it, manufacture weaponry manufactured material. On the surface, it looks normal, yet in the ground was a lot stored. Then, we used to go by underground train. It is true, the Russian train is the fastest and one of the wonders of the World. The constructed almost a mile down in the ground with a lot of electronic equipments. It's so fast, that if you do not watch out, before you turn around to signal your friend or companion that, the train is on the way, it would be already in your sight! It was really a great wonder which I consider it almost as fast as that of England. Only that, for the Russia, it covers fifty miles radius. It was fast when I learn Russian language and continued my lectures at the University. Within less than three (3) months to six ... but the time for me was enough to complete my certificate and started on my professional program.

The Uganda (Buganda) Kings' Representative (Owomutuba)... Edward Khiwa, kiwuwa.

Dr. Edward Khiwa, Kiwuwa addresses the group of his subjects on what it means to be a leader: leaders are persons who are able to influence others and who possess managerial authority. So, leadership is the ability to influence a group toward the achievement of goals. Three skills needed for a successful leader: i) conceptual skills... historical decisions making reflected by resume; ii)technical or academic skills and Human Relations skills. We are not born as leaders but, we learn from environment. Currently, I am the traditional leader representing the King of Buganda and help him to manage his subjects. In Kiganda language. I am called the Leader (the bark tree leader or kings subjects to lead and solve their needs on behalf of the king called in local language "Omutaka") who coordinates the affairs of the members of that clan.

There are fifty two clans and all of them are headed by the King of Baganda. The Baganda, reside in the central part of Uganda and their region is politically known as Buganda kingdom locally known as the kabaka of Buganda. Luyirika was a pure Muganda as the Baganda call a citizen of their own tribe. To be comfortable as a visitor in Uganda (Buganda) kingdom, you must belong to a kingdom's sub-clan headed by the king of Buganda kingdom. The king is the supremacy of the kingdom and any subject who holds a hereditary rank, has an important role in the eyes of the King of Buganda. I happened to hold this role and my presence is well felt before the people that call me their leader!

Edward Khiwa, Kiwuwa: the son of Erisa Luyirika the father of this great leader. The father of Luyirika from whom the son acquired the clan, belonged to Ndiga (Sheep animal) clan. In the tradition of Baganda, anybody born in this clan of heritage is supposed to be a brother and a sister to one another; regardless whether there is a history of maternal and paternal. Any one of that member is a very important person for the continuation of history of that family. They give their children the same names that could identify them from other fifty one clans. Such children do not marry each other and consider each other a member of the same family.

Members of the other fifty one clans do marry from Ndiga clan. As a result you could marry from other members of the clans. The practice has held and practiced by the Baganda as a ritual for many days of century. The consequences brought several folds advantage. One major of all, was that of belonging to one another as members of the same family.

The second advantages of belonging to a clan resulted in protecting such clan members from being infected of inherited diseases such as sickle cell anemia. The Luyirika's family could marry from other clans, except their own or the Ndiga clan. It is important for every Muganda (one member of the tribe of Baganad) clan to clearly understand their sources of origin and the leaders that have held their plight for years immemorial. The leaders of each clan have a ranking and respect bestowed by virtue of the knight the king of Buganda that gives to a selected leader of the clan an authority to represent him on all cultural functions. Such leader has a significant amount of authority. Leadership, authority and powers originate from that of supervising and bestowed the heir, and controlling the entire family during the time of death. The other power is that of management of the new birth in the family. The elder assigns the names of the new member in the family. Luyirika was assigned his names by his grand father. Then the Luyirika's off spring were given names by their grand father named Bayise. Of course Luyirika continued the practice by using the data of the existing list to assign names to his off spring. (6) Luyirika attended Mengo and Namukozi secondary schools both schools located in central geographical location of Buganda- Uganda. He was good in athletics, mathematics and English literature. He performed well in football or what others call Soccer game. He played the position of defending a goalie. He was an athlete who excelled in long distance jogging. He participated in civic debates. He had a good command of English language as such the missionaries and foreigners had to seek often for his English command as an interpreter for them into local vernacular languages.

Photo credit provided by the author.

The dowry price in Uganda, is a special moment when both parents of the girl expect to be rewarded for raising their daughter. On such event, all parties must wear long gown (kanzu): I was going to dowry moment and all were my siblings (Elder sister Victo Ntabade, Paul Kyaaka (eldest brother, myself, and others in my home family. We took alot of gifts, clothes and Money to give away. But, the event of real dowry was yet to come. Because of living in America, and the girl was in Uganda, it would have been impossible for her to wait for a year yet, she had others. Claire, how beautiful she was!

THE IMMIGRATION OF LUYIRIKA'S

As mentioned above, Luyirikas' have a historical ancestry home of origin from the central part of Uganda in the county Butambala a historical county concentrated of the Ndiga clan with citizens' background of Islamic population of believers.

The King of Buganda used to award administration of Butambala County to the Islamic with Moslem traditional practices. It was awarded to one of the members followers of Islam who fought aggressively in extension of the Kingdom of Buganda. Kibuuka was his name and as a reward for his triumph against the neighborly Kingdom (The Kitala) of Bunyoro. In recognition for his triumph, the leader whose of spring resulted in conquest of several counties that used to belong to Bunyoro gained the administration of the county as Katambala.

This was a reward to recognize the hard working soldiers of the pages of The Kingdom of Buganda (central part of the present Uganda) the residents of the county at that time, were now at the mercy of the leader of the county. They had to comply to his instructions; including their life styles practices. The most of all, they had to become a member of the Moslem community and of an Islamic belief. All residents had to comply with the leaders demand. If any resident had to violate the wishes of the county administrator, then he had to be forced to comply with all the traditions of the Islamic beliefs. This off course, included circumcision and respect of all Islamic beliefs and its traditions. A lot of people were forced to be

Moslems and as such could have access to properties and real estate of country side lands. If you did not own lands at that time, you could not be a ruler and could not be a leader of the clan; since land was a sign of wealth and anybody who had to squat on your land property had to pay you a monthly rent; and other interests to prove that you were a lovable and royal squatter. Majority of residents in that county at that time were not Moslems and had membership for several other missionary groups. A good number of county residents at that time belonged to either Church of Uganda or Roman Catholics.

The Church believers, whose church was sanctioned from the Church of England, were the majority in the country. The British government had a strong hold on Uganda at that time. It was its protectorate. But it had to use an indirect rule as for the people of the Kingdom of Buganda and Uganda as a whole. The Catholic missionaries also had a strong grip to its membership believers.

The Seventh Day Adventist missionaries arrived in Uganda in relatively the same time after. Off course, they arrived in Uganda in a small number following missionaries of the Church of Uganda/Church of England and the Catholic missionaries, headed by Pope moved aggressively to influence their beliefs to various members of the citizens of Uganda and Buganda at that time. Remember, that the name of Uganda was an extension by removing a prefix "B "from Buganda. It was done by Governor Cohen representing English Kingdom as to reward the King of Buganda for the good behavior of welcoming them warmly into his Kingdom. Actually, the British subjects at that time declared that they had met a Kingdom in the center of the Dark Continent that had the level of civics, judicial rule and leadership to that of England. They were very amazed for the level of civil administration that had never been anticipated to any part of the continent of Africa. While several Kingdoms in Uganda fought bitterly against the English missionaries on their arrival in Uganda; the Buganda Kingdom gave them a red carpet and welcomed them warmly. The nature of such civilization was of admiration to the British administration. The British government became friendly with Uganda due to the influence of Buganda King and leaders of its kingdom.

On the other hand, the English colonial governor of Uganda, since he had such a warm relationship, could not intervene in the decision making process made by the King of Buganda. In return, when King awarded Butambala County to the Moslems for fighting off the enemies, there were no repercussions and interventions that were brought upon the chief of the county to whom it had been awarded. The harassment against the residents of the non Moslem community in Butambara County continued and the King of Buganda did not stop it, neither did the English governor who had practiced an indirect rule for Uganda.

Consequently, several residents ran away from the county, and the grand parent of Luyirika; Kitanywa left in amidst of the struggle between the Moslem beliefs and non believers. Kitanwya the son of Ntambazi, who Luyirika recognized as his great, grand father, was never a member of Moslem community and an Islamic belief. Ntambazi the great- great father to Luyirika was moved in several grave yard tombs that the rest of his bones ended up put to rest in one of the corner of the county of Butambala. … Called "Bweeya". In Uganda there is a saying if something is very large: that it's large as to the extent of "Bule and Bweeya."

Meaning that, the region between these two pieces of land, were of a lot of bones of contentions that resulted in the stiffness to the residents of the same county. Off course it is a difference of about sixty miles from one side of the county to another and members of that county belong to the same clan. Njogeza a son of Ntambazi the conqueror of the enemies for that county split with his brother Mpungu Banadawa and developed Bweeya and since then, we have the demarcation caused by two brothers who had different religious philosophy; but causing the reef in the county politics and administration.

However, the confrontations of the off spring in the children of the same family, became a land of demarcation that the children born in Buule to a father "nick named Banadawa … Mpungu, "also a son of Ntambazi who was a stout Moslem, decided to own a mile of land on which his off spring were born, buried and inherited as well keeping the Islamic beliefs and its traditions. On the side of Bweeya the children of Ntambazi also owned lands and properties that; the county remained in the strong hold of the Ndiga (sheep animal) clan. Of course, the county as of today is made up of residents who are not necessarily of Islamic background. The record indicates that even if Kitanywa moved in several places of Buganda Kingdom including the location on Masaka road, his final place of rest was at Bweeya (famous warrior place for the second world war II) the great grand father was a hero since the white colonial administrators of Uganda, drafted him to go frontline and fought in areas of the far east Asia, on their behalf. Several young men at that time, were recruited to join the army and were sent to face the enemies of the colonial leaders of Uganda. They liked these young men, because, they were from the equatorial and had experience with the rainy weather and tropical temperatures than the whites who were virtually new in the tropical and equatorial lands. My grand was given a crush course of how to shoot using a gun and pistol and safeguarding from the enemies. After, ending the Second World War II, he and the surviving military young men were brought back on the ship and crossed the east African waters of the Indian Ocean and came back by train, cargoes and arrived back to his home land Uganda. He was welcomed back in glory since none of his family had ever gone that far abroad, not to mention the return home back alive from the scavenger of foreign wars. He was called a brilliant leader and was offered a piece of land in Mityana, central part of Uganda. The King of Buganda appointed him the leader of his subjects since now he had proved that he had the skills of leadership and of royal to the king and the colonial leader. The Mikaya Bayise, Waswa, as his names were, enjoyed the new land that he had been given by the king, he ended up residing in it with both his children, "Erisa Luyirika and his brother and his wife." Until he died in his given land. In the words of the first daughter of Luyirika: the grand father told his children and off springs that, "the land is capital and wealth, and that there is nothing worth to live for than protecting the land, that land is our Mother and we should protect it and no one should ever take it away from us. No one should ever sell the land. It is a hereditary property where no one should ever overpower it and take it from my grand children. Also, in his Will, he mentioned that, he had to be buried in that piece of land that was given to him by his King and the colonial leaders of the county at that time. They gave it to him as a gift of his triumph and memories to his being a hero.

The Luyirikas' are proud of their origin since their father is traceable from the great-great parents of Buule, to a place called Ndegye in Kyadondo County…. A place where his great parents had responsibilities to prepare Kings Brewery that was served in the palace at that time. Kyadondo County is pre-dominantly the seat of the administration of Buganda Kingdom, and the Federal Government of Uganda.

As noticed, Luyirika and his father were not members of Moslem beliefs, neither did any of his other parents. Although, a majority of his family were Islam. Luyirika's family escaped being turned into Islam as the county from which he was born had been given to all Islamic believers. The executive order of the county administrator, came down to all chiefs in county to circumcise all boys and their parents who were not Islam. A good many residents at that time in the county, had to run away in the middle of the night before the executive order put into practice. The running away at night, meant also to confront wild beasts on the way since the country was wild and no roads. The people had to hide in the bush, beaches, forestry, and had to hide and move quietly to avoid being noticed while saving their lives. My grandfather, with his father, managed to escape to another safe counties and escaped torture and death; for many people did not survive after the award of the county to the Moslem and when the executive order from the governor of the county was announced and had to be implemented to keep on controlling the county as an Islamic county. The religious battles in Africa, cause the continent frontiers of a political parties. The benefits and promotions is based on the side of religion you believe in. This is centrally, to western world's way of thinking. However, the conditions in Africa, as you visit in each country, you will observe religious institutions based on their home of the former colonial powers of heritance. The struggle and confrontation of religious leaders due to their former colonial headquarters, is one of the colonial legacy that has kept the continent in constant wars within amongst nations. For instance, in Africa, the side of religion you are on, also means the supporters will give you votes because they consider you, one of their own. Another, weakness brought by the colonial to Africa is the destruction of the local traditional values. They promulgated values such as imported culture of languages, English, French, and many more languages that replaced the African and local traditional values. Colonials brought the enforcement of the Bible a sole document for human values and forced the local communities to forego theirs. The rules and laws the colonial leaders left to the continent as a legacy has left a lot desired. Questions are being raised, did the colonial period of arrival to places in Africa, cause difference in civilization of the continent or it kept to the level of civilization to that of the former colonials! What if the colonial administrators did not come to discover continent would the African nations not be better off! It is argued, that the colonial leaders benefited more in partitioning the lands of Africans than the Africans benefited of their arrivals. Of course, whose culture do we measure civilization? Is civilization a domain of a certain group of people to dominate the subservient of culture of others? Does exploitation with a method of importing a culture, lead to civilization of another community? Instead, it destroys the achievements, the level of history that community would have achieved. When you destroy a language, and you replace the local languages with foreign say English, you automatically destroy civilization of that community. Africans have plenty to feel proud of what would have united all of them as one and make it a strong Continent. African values were destroyed. African like other nations had potential to use their basic natural gifts and develop their own values and institutions. In comparative time, Africa was dominated when the colonials were fighting in their countries.

If Africa had been left alone, it would have prospered to use its own cultural values and languages to the point of fixing their own educational, Universities, as according to their natural history. The countries that have ignored outside influence, and defended their cultural languages are today are better off than those whose current languages are imported from abroad. For instance, nations such as Japan, Russia, China, France, Scandinavian nations their civilization is paved due to using their natural culture and uninterrupted mother tongue.

    The African nations would benefit more today, if they restore more of their historical values and use less glorification of the imported culture. The western world, by spearheading through the African continent, they managed to build themselves castles such as "the capital of England; France etc. There is still ample time to restore the lost glories and heritages. African countries and others in the same class, should defend themselves from foreign and immigration cultural interference. National civilizations and Kingdoms have disappeared because they were excessively kind to allow, and accepted foreign culture as one of their own. Ultimately, the institutions were weakened and the kingdoms were destroyed. A typical example are those of the South America, i.e. Aztecs, the Amayo etc. They are today, off the global. On contrary, the World today is a global village with its latest inventions of technology of the 21st Century… causing such communication network of internet WebCT's etc. We need to regulate the internet machinery network from exploiting young generations causing abusive civilization of technology we are proud of in the integration of the global community. Nations such as Sweden have held a constant conservative culture, and advanced civilization with modern technology. They did not give off their own, and yet the country has received thousands of immigrants across its boarder. The Kingdom of Buganda in Africa, has lived for over five hundred years, and yet, has held high the traditional vernacular language of, "Luganda" spoken and understood by about 87% of the population in Uganda. The people in kingdom like their king and as such his policies and cultural implementation is easy to carry out and defend against foreign influences. That is the extent of longevity of development and proud of it for the subjects of the Kingdom. The Kingdom struggles to defend against cultural exploitation of outside communities. As it struggles to achieve its total independence by improving its political system to become a more decentralized system, it will regain the glory which was destroyed by former leaders that did not like kingdoms in Uganda. But, Buganda kingdom, is a module of many nations that are protecting their own values and cultural civilization.

Luyirikas' as intellectual moving families:

The Luyirikas' moved on from place to place. That is in understanding the history of the Luyirikas', it is important to study all the basis of his heritage. His connection with the roots of Buule and Bweeya was of due reason that his great father Ntambazi, had a son "Mpungu, Banadawa, who was the father of Saad Kafumbe that grew together with Erisa Luyirika. Saad Kafumbe although was a Moslem by belief, he played a major role in uniting the family of "Mpungu Banadawa. His role of uniting the family of Balengera another grand father of Erisa Luyirika, improved a great awareness of the history of his heritage. Balengera was a son of Ntambazi. It may be remembered that Kakomo was the father of Kirigendali who was the father of Ntambazi, the father of Mpungu–Banadawa (nick named), who was the father of some of the selected children such as Saad Kafumbe, Al jab Kyaaka, Musoke Nasibu Njogeza, Kakomo, Nasereka, and Kayima. More family members are being investigated as of writing this memorobia. It is of paramount to recognize the Baganda tradition of Mutuba a sub unit of Siga (major sub clan). The present Buule sub unit is under the management of "Katangaza" under the care taker of the living father Kayima. It used to be under management of Abbey Kafumbe the successor to elder Saad Kafumbe, the son of Mpungu Banadawa. Apparently, the Omutuba of Katangaza belonged in the management line of the Luyirikas' by virtue of the tradition of management of Ntambazi heritage. However, the great grand father of Mpungu- Banadawa, took over as a care taker since the rest moved out of the county and especially they never owned a real estate in that county one of the requirements of Muluka leadership. Though, Luyirikas' heritage belonged to Katangaza, it was supposed to be the leadership guide for the ancestry of Ntambazi. On the other hand, the line of Musoke one of the families from Mpungu Banadawa qualified to have its own Mutuba and it was named "Lwasa Mitala" and being managed by Ali- Mpungu of Seeta / Bweeya in Butambala. Ali-Mpungu is also the His eminent high ranking prime minister (Katikiro) of the leader of Ssiga Highest reign next to the leader of Ndiga clan, his name is Bosa.) At present, there are two Mituba from the same Lujja (ranking of family) an indication of the growth of the family. At present there is virtually no proper administration for "Katangaza" since the care taker to Abbey Kafumbe is not established. Until that is clear, there is no leader in that position. Abbey Kafumbe successor was a care taker, but his successor to continue the legacy of leadership as a care taker is not yet elevated.

THE OLD MAN AND HIS FINAL WORDS OF WISDOM

My journey from USA to Uganda during President IDD Amin's turmoil government.

In 1980 the author left Uganda for USA. He did not realize that it was going to turn out to be his last holiday with his Daddy and Mom. The trip was not planned as usual and as with others. It was a season of political turmoil in Uganda. The incumbent president was facing inside political unrest, and the governments of international community had committed to see that he had to vacate the office. The international financial agencies boycotted offering loans and the investors were agitated to spend any dollar in Uganda. Inflation plumaged to a rate high than it had ever been in history of Uganda. There was civil unrest every where in the country. There were massive demonstrations in some parts of the country and nationals abroad but were responded with firing arm and imprisonment. The nation was going through unabated challenges of human rights and as such the mood in the country was jilt to both foreigners and the local nationals. There were suspicious behaviors of non nationalism, that the government and its president was uncomfortable to govern since at any time, a wind of politics supported by a foreign power could move in and a new government had eminent to be installed. Being scared of a fellow citizen over another was much in line as a day by day event of life.

Mikaya Bayise, the father of Erisa Luyirika and the grandfather of the author of The Days of Outlives. This man was recognized as one of the best in fighting with sniper gun that killed a lot of enemies against the English and the local wars in Uganda. Locally was called as "Bakawonawo." War survivors. He lived up to 117 years before he died and is said to have lived amongst the longest of his time.

The government was scared of the foreigners in anticipation that they were potential spies and rival to the citizens of Uganda. Warnings had been put out by United States Department of State to stay away from Uganda. Therefore, for the author to start a journey to Uganda was an act not of a timid but a genuine character. The author recognized that, probably anything could happen while he was at home. There was no choice but he had to fly to Uganda to participate in the funeral rites of elder brother Kizza who had died. He had to meet the challenge. Kizza raised him and contributed tremendous finances for his academic education. He had been advised by a foreign student colleague from Kenya not to venture Uganda at that height of political mighty. Kenya is a neighborly country to Uganda and the student had a brother that had just left Uganda but was then posing advice from Nairobi Kenya to students in East Africa studying in USA.(7)

In any case, regardless of the warning, the author made up his minds and planned to travel a three day's flight from US to Entebbe air port in Uganda in East Africa. On arriving in Nairobi Kenya, a brother of his friend with whom they were students in US advised him to live off important documents to his brother's home in Nairobi, Kenya before traveling by bus a five hundred miles stony and unpaved tarmac road inside the country of Uganda. It was a move carefully planned. He did the same. When I arrived in Nairobi, I telephoned Mr. Ochen the brother of my friend to meet me at the Airport and set up a strategy of how I could arrive in Uganda's Capital, Kampala.

I lived in his home for four days while both of them were investigating and studying conditions in the neighborly nation of Uganda. It was not easy to conduct surveillance from a five hundred miles away of the capital of destination that's, Nairobi to Kampala. All indications from the travelers coming by either bus or plane from Uganda, was that the life and conditions were futile for the citizens and foreigners inside the country, especially traveling from overseas. Mr. O Chen however conducted much of the investigation while on the Kenya side. Visitors who were coming from Uganda to Nairobi by Akamba bus (a Kenya national bus), advised people not travel to Uganda.

The author however, had to check with Uganda envoy and counselor from Uganda stationed in Nairobi, Kenya, who advised against visiting Kampala at that time. But, if any body had absolutely had to go there, a lot of precautions had to be taken against the insurgents of Uganda government. The author was now put on high tension. The Uganda envoy mentioned also that if amongst of us were to be a foreigner from say, an enemy supporting country such as USA, it would be a big and a major risk since the immigration border check points had been put on alert for suspicious and dubious citizens and foreigners coming far away beyond the neighboring countries. The author became more disdained against government of his home country.

It had been reported that a truck was packed by the boarder between Kenya and Uganda to pick up every able body that could be trained for the military to fight against the enemies. The truck was packed at boarder entrance at 8:00 Am. and would not be moved away until it was full of able fighting boys and men. As long as you were a man and boys you had to be picked up and board the truck bounding the training military barracks. There were no excuses that could be honored whatsoever. All were done under the disguise of defending the country. The days were of sorrow and could be visible on citizens' eyes.

he military guarding the Uganda–Kenya boarder also were aware that their days of being alive were numbered and could be taken to front line to fight against the enemies' weapons. They were scared of each other and worse of all they were picked up every morning to go fight the enemies. There was new military security selected to man the boarder virtually every morning. They never new each other and who would be their boss the next morning. It was kept that way to eliminate potential collaborators within military ranks and management.

EDWARD KHIWA, PHD

THE MOMENT OF SILENCE; A EIGHTY MILE FROM THE BORDER TO KAMPALA

After seven hours of waiting against "panda gali" means (climbing the military truck by force); that's waited for the military truck to leave, then a Kenyan resident who lives at the boarder, whom the author paid to conduct surveillance and to monitor the Uganda military activities at the boarder (off course) he finally gave the author a word of "get ready".. The author had given him security advance sum of money to watch the situation on his behalf.

After the truck had been driven away, my king and friend told me that, that was the time to move in and cross the Kenya-Uganda border. Fortunately, he had his house which was partially his shop just close to the border of Kenya-Uganda. He begged to get ready to cross the boarder into Uganda for the military truck had just disappeared from the military and security guards. The author new at that time that now his life was in danger, but he had to risk and cross the boarder after passing through the government Hench men. He had to make a move. The Kenyan citizen at the boarder cautioned that this was a very high risk journey. "You have to go and see your people, your parents and the rest of nieces and nephews since they had now turned orphans as their father had died due to conditions of the environment and political climate of the country." At first the author was reluctant to venture the Uganda military boarder guard. With hesitation he collected stamina and headed the boarder. The military through instructions was very angry against foreign governments which were supporting the overthrow of their government. Of all nations anger was turned against was United States of America that was giving military and financial support to the rebel that was antagonizing the current government of Uganda.

In any case the author had to create courage and move towards the Uganda boarder. Before the author could move on, the idea came to him: "The guard and military men are hungry, why don't you give them something to eat" The minds talked to me. It was 2:00 p.m and the sun could melt ice in less than a second. The sun of the equator had a high temperature that had to force every one outside to have a sip of water every half an hour. The day was hot as a fire. The majority of people were walking with no clothes on their backs. Some were walking with knickers and half bottom clothes due to the heat of the day.

The author had to do something. The author had been cautioned that the public bus transportation heading to Uganda was about to leave and was the last on that day. The author was now about 80 miles from the Capital of Uganda–Kampala, a town that had not seen him for twenty years. Though he was raised in it, the author had left it for study over seas when he was a teenager.

The idea came to me to provide feeding of the military guard. I had a basket that was full of my clothes while leaving capital city of Nairobi Kenya, so, I used my basket to solve the puzzle for me. Remember that, the moment the Kenya bus stopped I was right at the border with Kenya and Uganda; all passengers heading to Uganda were on their own. The passengers that did not hold back" a wait and see", were forced into the military truck, locally known as "panda Gali" meant, climb the truck and swing wherever it was heading in the battlefield. They had come from long journeys as I was. Some had come from Scandinavians nations, Europeans, Australia and others were Ugandans had come to Kenya to shop and go home, while those from a far, had come for vacation and to see their families and relatives. They did not know that, travelling in bus at night, and arriving at the Kenya-Uganda boarder that night in the morning, was the fate of their lives. When the Kenyan bus stopped at the boarder, they hurriedly jumped out to go to Uganda, their home country of origin. To a disappointment, and with all their tiredness of sitting in the Bus, that had to gallop up and down on the un tarmac roads, were greeted to arrive Uganda with a beatings to climb the trucks that were already waiting for the travelers such as them to go to wars and fight the enemies of the government of President of Uganda Mr. Obote and his government. Without notice, the travelers to Uganda at that early morning hours at eight o'clock, were shortly, helped to climb the bus, and loaded them to a field and were given a two hour training in gun shooting and then way assigned to fight the enemies on the front line.

A lot of people died. They faced enemies they did not know, and heard. The leadership and ruthless behavior of the government of Uganda at that time, scared the arrivals to Uganda and others around the World.

On my side, then, I did not hurry to cross the Kenya- Uganda boarder. I was nervous, and timid. I stayed at the small shop at the side of Kenya's boarder. There, I had met a sympathizer of all of us. He had known that, crossing the border from Kenya to Uganda, at that time at eight in the Morning, would be a fate and would be the last hour of life. He cautioned me to be careful and monitor my movements at the boarder.

Meantime, while stranded at this small local shop at the boarder, I prayed within myself. I had come along way, and had been to Uganda for over ten years. The government was at keen to those who were travelling from America since it was supporting the rival faction of the enemy against the government. After standing with shivering in the corner of the local shop, I could not bear what I had to do then! Thoughts came and go! Should I go back to Kenya and then forth to America? Or what should be the best approach to solve my crisis?

Stranded, with nothing that should appear and resemble coming from a foreign lands, especially America, an idea visited me! For even the small boarder shop man, had began to antagonize me that the end of life was just about to begin. He was however, using his microscope to determine when the trucks would leave with their victims and vacate the boarder! Yes, a certain idea came to me when he told me that the trucks with their live human body victims, had started to live and suddenly, all of them, cleared the boarder, except the policemen, and the military border patrol. I figured it out soon, "it was now my time to go to cross Uganda boarder. But, how would I face these blood thirsty militia policemen, and body guard patrol? Remember, I was single and alone with no ID on myself.

The language of the boarder at that time, was Swahili. But, my Swahili of third and fourth grade, did not carry wait to those high powered technician of Swahili speakers border patrol. I knew that, English would put me in danger since many of them, could not speak English for they had a grade four drop out educational literacy. Speaking a language they could not hear and understand, would mean to them being embarrassed and undermining them. This would bring to me a severe punishment that I would never forget. So, my new Kenyan friend on Kenya boarder wondered how I would solve this crisis.

Then, there was another problem, to being noticed a foreigner from a foreign land. I had all the symptoms of a foreigner: First, I was healthy, stout, charm, big smile, handsome young man, tall, with all features of an athletic and college material from United States. There was no where to hide. My accent in speaking English was not of an Englishman, but an American. The style of talk was that of executive. So, they would soon notice. By the way, at that time, I had developed an infectious life. What a life challenge that I was!

Amazingly, during the moment of waiting for the clear time to cross the boarder, I bought a few items on the market at the side of Kenya–Uganda boarder.

My little Kenyan friend, with a small boarder shop on Kenya side, was now very busy with his inventions: the microscopic to monitor all the movements I would be going through as a new challenge to Uganda. I will admit, that, this was first time to come to the boarder side of Uganda from my central district of Uganda. The languages spoken by people at Uganda boarder were not familiar at all! The distance of about five hundred miles from my home did not make it easy for me. But, then, I would not fly to Uganda, since it was more risky than coming on land by bus. That's' how I came at the border with Kenya. My Kenyan friend advised me not to look smart but, a bit of intelligent.

In a moment of notice, my friend came back from the other side of Uganda boarder and told me to get ready that, every thing had now been set in mood to move in and sit in the passenger bus that had just come to pick up the survivors at the Kenyan-Uganda boarder.

When it was now time to venture to cross to Uganda, I hurriedly parked ripened bananas, cooked maize or corn, roasted cassava and peanuts that I had purchased at the boarder of Kenya-Uganda, and covered the food with clothes that I had with in the basket, that I had planned to wear when I arrive Uganda.

Of course, they were not clothes of high rank, but old jeans, torn away dirty courts and shirts. I used them to look as if I was one of the local residents of the boarder that deals in trade, at regular bazaar seasons, and that, I made the patrol police to think that I was a residence on the side of Kenya- Uganda boarder since Uganda policemen, could not pick up on the Kenyan residents..

I covered more clothes on top of Corn outside of the basket. I, then put on top of a basket a batch of ripe bananas, roasted cassava, and peanuts. Since the Uganda Kenya boarder had a local bazaar trade market; by carrying the basket on my head, and was full of food, at that sunny day, the military boarder management, had to ask for food.

They were not being fed enough and not on time as my Kenyan friend had revealed to me. Soon as possible, I came to their stop over for check point, I willingly shared with them, what I had, had on my head, as I was crossing the boarder towards the passenger bus to Uganda.

Yes, the police and military check up points, were very happy and hungry indeed to see a man who was holding a basket on his head, but, full of food. Actually, they thought that I had been selling goods and services at local bazaar market on that day. Apparently, they went along and accepted my invitation to share with them my basket food. Along with their wishes, I joined them by speaking my broken Swahili language. I passed also food to their army commander, so that he could keep himself and his company happy. Oh yes, they were exceedingly happy. They were very happy for sharing what had been given to them.

Quietly, I bade goodbye in my broken Swahili, and they promised to look after me, since they had thought that, I was a local trader of the local market. I promised them to give them more food. They were being served nothing or a little bean and little porridge, was one served to them the whole day. They were happy to eat for nothing!

Actually in their minds they thought that I was a residential neighborhood. I put on, local clothes and had no foreign visible clothes, and my clothes were no different from a trader in that market. Fortunately, the bus on bound to Kampala was parked and boarding for Kampala… an 80 mile journey. Good enough, it did not take long and the bus was soon parked full of passengers on bound to Uganda.

The bus driver, stopped over one stage and that was at Jinja municipal town. We stayed over that town for a half an hour and until, they set us to another fifty miles to Kampala. The period I was away, the new properties had turned many years old. Of course everything appeared new before my eyes. As we crossed the country side, I noticed, the country side roads, rugged and very old. The buildings did not have maintenance, rehabilitation and many of the houses were falling a part. The civil war in the countryside, had taken away all resources and stamina for people to fix anything. They were expecting death at any moment! The fellow passengers looked timid all the time and were scared of each other's conversation.

So the bus was quiet most of the time. The form of wearing revealed the people had no money and conditions were continually poor. People looked pale, slim and weak. Did the driver know what he was doing? He drove the bus at a high speed in anticipation to avoid potential military rebels on the way. The country was in the civil war. Sometimes, bullets would pass over the bus we were in. Rumblings of gun shots could be heard on our way to the Capital of Uganda. The driver started driving from the boarder at 3:00 p.m., but because of so many check points, I thought we would never arrive and stay at the road forever. On the way, I saw littered dead bodies thrown side by side on the road and highways. Dead bodies with bullets wounds and soldiers with machine guns and walkie talkie had been decorated their clothes with green forestry leaves and behaved like warriors. We got stopped on the way by the military soldiers who had the same attire, we had to stop with no questions asked. Several times we had to get out of the bus and kneel down under the orders of their commander. We were often asked to pull out everything we had in our pockets. Some of our fellow travelers were left there, they were beaten and hung on ropes and strings, tied together in ramshackle but with a thread of lock we picked up ourselves and a shock we stepped back in the bus and we resumed our journey leaving our fellow travelers behind. The people who were left behind had answered the military that they're on their way from other countries and it was a threat to IDD Amin's government. After a little while driving we had gun shots in the air and machine guns near the place we just left. The bus driver increased the speed to 120 miles per hour to avoid the rebels on the way, it was a challenge to our lives because I remember my travel mate on the bus, he had given me a note to pass it to his family. I gave it to his family after a few days and they told me that he didn't make it to Kampala capital of Uganda. He was a highly educated man with all his credentials and was a great loss to the country and the world.

Finally, we arrived Kampala at 7: 00 p.m. and straight away, I took a taxi and moved in to the house of my family life friend and brother. He had been for many years a family friend. I could trust him to live with him and his family. At night, rumblings of gun shots could be heard everywhere in the City. You had to have a gun to control your homestead, and family from being panicked. People never slept in their homes. They hid in the bush and big trees and anywhere they could find shelter. Some of them had to sleep in the chimney and had their bedroom up there. When stealing was taking place, they could force people to open their homes and any hesitation would amount to gun shooting and property stolen. Sometimes, the thugs could come in the home and tie the homeowner with ropes and rape his wife and daughters. Then some time would leave them either dead or disabled. The departure of Idi Amin and president Obote was a great struggle and only a survival for the lack and fittest could meet with a new government.

I did not sleep the night I arrived in capital. The security was a challenge. The next morning I took a bus towards countryside to visit my parents I had not seen for twenty years. It were the City within Central Uganda called Mityana where my ancestral parents' home had been situated. It was a distance of 40 miles west of the capital of Uganda. But, on the way, you could notice dead bodies hit by the bullets lying on the roadside.

On the other hand, there was a sigh of relief when my mother show me at a distance. My mother screamed at the top of her mouth and called father who was cutting grass in the farm. When my father heard the scream of his wife, or my mother, he too hurriedly ran as fast as his legs could carry him and came and embraced me with a great hug of welcome. "Welcome back my baby" my father cried. "God can now call me home as I have seen you", my mother exclaimed. They quietly went into the house and father commanded as usual to kneel down and thank God for leading me into their lives when they were still alive. They were definitely turning old and were walking bent with sticks. They had been disabled as they had fractured themselves from falls of picking cotton and running after cattle and goats. They could hardly perform duties in the same way I had left them before I went to study in Russia to carry on further education.

Revision Questions

1. What is the most source of happiness for a parent?
2. Why do most leaders in developing countries, do not vacate leadership chairs and or presidency in time expected?
3. How should developing nations determine the fate of their independence?
4. Did the colonial leaders deprive their subjects the right to learn to be true governors of their independence?
5. How should civilized community protect their civilization?
6. Who feel the most memory of loneliness; a child who never show parents dead at the last minute, or those that had a chance to bid farewell to their parents until death?

CHAPTER III

FATHER REVEALS OUR HERITAGE THE NIGHT EVE OF DEPARTURE FROM UGANDA

It was turning 5:00 am when the author heard mother and father conversing in their bed room. Of course each parent had his/her bed.

Joshua Kigeya Kamya sitting with his younger brother Timothy Bayise in the black suit. Joshua was the successor and leader of the estate of Erisa Luyirika the center of the family at Namakofu in central Uganda, Africa; he now carries out the legacy of his father.

They were very happy couple and had to talk every moment at night about several subjects. Now they new that their boy was about to leave for USA, so they called him in their bed room that morning when every one of their grandees and children sleeping. Father called him first, but he hesitated. Then mother cried out aloud and said, "your father is calling you, come out of your bed; he wants to tell you a few things." The boy had to obey mother so he walked up when every one in the home was deep a sleep except: mother, father, and myself. Father told his boy to kneel by his bed side. Across was his mother's bed. Father started in a low mood and voice. Mother cried out, and said to father, "speak louder so your son will hear you" She lamented to her husband also who was the author's father! His father started to tell him his roots and the family roots. He mentioned that as days folded, you children had to know the history of your heritage. He said that the oldest brothers and sisters in the family that would have taken you to your family roots had died many years ago and yet you the young one did not know your heritage. He said, "We come from Bweeya and Bule" in Butambala county in central part of Uganda. He mentioned that, "my son, I want you when you come back tell your brothers and sisters, that, our heritage is Bule and Bweeya." He cautioned his son that his brothers were of Moslem beliefs, but others were of different faiths but that did not make any difference as far as he was concerned. He mentioned to his son that "we are seventh day Adventists, but this is only a religion and belief of faith. The religion is something important but is equally important as your blood family. He said that", the family book that is lying by the table on my bed, carries in it very important information which will lead you to your grand parents. "He lamented, "your family is made of the believers of seventh day Adventists and your true blood families that come from Bule and Bweeya are not". He said, "When you come back from your studies abroad "I want you to look for your brothers and sisters and may be grand papa. "But, for us we are going you will not meet us again." I doubt it because the bodies have grown weak day by day. At Bule and Bweya is where my history of origin. "My child, he asked, do you know any body other than the church members?"

WHAT MY FATHER TOLD ME AT THREE IN THE MORNING

The boy replied, he would not know if you his daddy could not tell him. "Well my son, it is too late. You are today boarding for U.S a place we have never and had never expected to educate our child. You have impressed me and you have given glory to the family. "You and your big brother Joshua have done an extraordinary. In the same way I want you to go mile further than any body else and extend your arm to my family at Bule and Bweeya and Entebe and others where they could be found. It is because I committed to my faith, but you children could have seen many more of your family blood. I regret that this has not happened. The book should tell everything as you discover one by one of your family blood". He continued.

Never mix religion with blood. We are different but we are the same. Our relationship to one another is a bond made of our family relations. It will be difficult to sort out your family at Bule and Bweeya and Entebe and some members on the Kobe Island where I have never been before. But remember this is your family. Never allow religion of whatever level and intensity to separate you from each other. You are one blood. It is unfortunate that I could not take you to my brothers and family. I was appointed to be Omutuba (leader clan). But the religion could not give me moment to meet with my blood family. However, I am happy even though you may not see me again, "go and search for your family on my behalf, and do what I should have done when I am alive. Never separate from your religion. This is the true religion and the way that will lead us to one another. Never drink beer and wine and never smoke. When I asked, who in Bule and Bweya to look for? He mentioned several names but he seemed to have heard that some of them had died. But mentioned the names any way: Saad Kafumbe was pointed out as they grew together, yet he was older than him by about ten. He mentioned Kyaka; Mustaffa son of Balengera but was raised by Mpungu Banadawa, Yokana Kinobe. But he could not remember many details. He had remembered Lwasa mitala Musoke. He mentioned the line of Banadawa Mpungu. He said that man was a true representative of the family of Ntambazi. The boy asked him who his father was, to which he said that was Mikaya Bayise and that was burried in the same place of his home; he said his wife was Nalongo.

He said his grand father was Kitanywa. The boy did not have any more stamina to follow up more. But the author asked him about Entbbe to which he replied that Balengera was his grand father as was Ntambazi. The conversation again changed to a different areas; the boy did not care asking him questions such as Omutuba, Saza, Kasolya etc because they did not make sense to him and he had never heard of them. He told him that some of his family members migrated from Bweeya and Bule to Ndejje (kyadondo). More details on this subject was pending he could see him crying and his eyes were getting wet. He again repeated: "my child love your brothers and sisters when ever find them regardless of their religion, that way you will be strong and you will be famous as a family. Never discriminate, and always show courage to the stand for your decision. Remember to encourage your fellow brothers whenever you found them that they should stay strong. He finally said: "My son, always remind your family to stay strong in the religion of their fathers and grand fathers. Never try to convert them, for they are your brothers who have their values. You should respect each one's faith and remind them that it is because of the faith of their parents and grand parents that the family is strong. Let us respect each other's philosophy of faith. He cautioned that if you deal fairly with one another, not converting each other but to accommodate, you will be well respected by many members of your clans including those who are not! (8)

Luyirika's roots …. "KIKONGE'S": The Great-Great Parents of Luyirika (2nd great parent and the next kin in line)

Kikonge the proprietor and the leading heritage of the children of the sub –clan called "Katangaza" or in local language in Uganda, it means "a long range of lightness and sun shine in the darkness." The great –great father of Luyirika had several children that he raised. They are as follow: Manyabigambo; Tanyikala; Nabitula; and Munakuwazo.

Kikonge had several children amongst of them was his son named:

Nantagya- Mpungu. It should be recalled that, Kikonge or Nkonge as some people called him, was one of the sons of Mpungu the leader of the Ndiga sub clan.

Nantagya's children: Nantagya was the first son of (Kikonge) Nkonge.

Mbwanango, Sewagudde, Sepiriya Lugeya, Benikito Kiwuwa (lived at Bugozi in Budu county of Buganda, central Uganda), Namubiru, Nkonge at Kyanukuzi, Buddu County.

Terata, Alibaka, Alibala i.e Nabutono, Petero Wakulira, Ndegeya.

Sepiriya Lugeya the eldest son of Ki (konge), had next in kins (Brothers and sisters). Some of them are discussed below.

B. They are as follow: Kitanywa, and Balengera (it should be mentioned that, these children, when old men moved from place to place with their families and did not stay in a place for along time. However, it may also note that, the wars of the Butambala of the Islamic religion and non-Moslem believers.

Kitanywa's children: Vunyi, Sirasi Kiwuwa, Namala, Lwenyaga the father of Yusuf and still lives (By the time of writing in 2007),

MORE ABOUT KIKONGE (Our great great grand father) Our grand father Kikonge, is the sole grand father we know of all time. He is the first grand father we have in records in which we all spring. He is the only one and the first one we currently remember.

Kajongolo — never had a child

Nantagya – Mpungu (His first child)

Balengera

Batwerinde (the twin brother of Balengera)

Sirasi Kiwuwa

Kitanywa Kiwalata never had a child and finally,

Kuli Omuyaga who too never had a child. Kikonge was buried at Bulwee.

KITANYWA: (1st grand father to Luyirika) The home of this grandfather was at Katende. His successor was Kiwuwa. This honorable man was buried at Nakabiso, and his grave side, there is a great big tree. His tomb is under a big tree in Buganda is called, "Gwafu."

Mbwanago his son did not have a child. (Was buried at Bugonzi) in Budu county, in Buganda kingdom. The son of Bakigadya at Kyagwe, succeded him.

Kitanywa's mother: Zikuzza was Kikonge's wife and the mother of Kitanwa. Kitanwya was buried at Nakabiso, and the following are his children (Kitanywa's children):

Loza (Rose) Nnakimbugwe. She died at Namunyanyula

Vunyi his mother was Namukasa and Vinyi was buried at Mbale.

Mikaya Bayise (Waswa) and his sister Nakato

Maliya Namirembe. This Luyirika's auntie was burried in Bulemezi in a village called "Bulinde." In the midst of her children. Janet the Nakibuuka the daughter of Yonasan Musoke succeeded her.

Kyaka, this one died at Bule. The five had the same mother. She was called "Namukasa."

Ntabade died at Kirya Muli. She died from death of her first child.

Kyakuuma died at Luvumbula

Kagwa went in exile and did not come back.

Namazi and

Ndegeya all and the

Boy who died an infant.

Namanya: this one died at Luvumbula. She was the wife of Kitanwa and had the following children:

Kigeya or Kamya and

Kiterera who was burried at Luvumbula and

Kakomo who died of Musaamya and died while at Nakatema, Namusote when had just died. She died of last child. Both the old and the young died together.

Munaku: (Kitanywa's wife) the second wife of Kitanywa. Munaku the second wife of Kitanywa Who died at Bwebaja, bore the following children for her husband Kitanywa: Zawedde died at Bwebajja in Buganda and

Nabigujju who died at Kibuye

NAKATUDDE and Siras Kiwuwa the successor to kitanywa.

Kitanywa's home was at Katende.

At Katende, he had the following children except Siras Kiwuwa who was born at Mpanga (near namakofu) and Mr. Yonasan Musoke succeeded Siras Kiwuwa). *Siras Kiwuwa the successor of Kitanywa) – had only one child and her name was Namala.*

Vunyi:

Vunyi was Kitanywa's son and he had a wife called "Nsonga."

Vunyi had the following children: i). Sewagudde 2). The 2nd died young 3) serubiri Semion.... All his children died. He too was buried at Mulago, and the 4th died at Mbale.

MIKAYA BAYISE WASWA (Twin brother & Nakato whose lineage is not clear, but under further investigation)

His wife was Gwalibawade and the following was the history of his birth of children:

Erisa Luyirika the eldest and

Mikayiri Nanfumba the youngest.

Mikaya Bayise had only two children. (Erisa Luyirika & Michael Nanfumba) Luyirika was the eldest and succeeded him and has the estate at Namakofu and so, was his young brother Nanfumba, both were buried at Namakofu).

Mikaya Bayise their father, was buried at Namakofu in his estate located near Kyaka who died at Bule ... did not have children.

- KIGEYA (Kitanywa's son) Kigeya his wife was called Naggwa (was burried across the street from Yonasani Musoke's home) Kigeya was the father of the following children:
  - Yonasani Musoke Walung'ama of Namakofu (died at Mulago hospital)
  - Yozefu Kiwanuka whom he had in his sister (Nakatude). The child was taken to Nandere Roma catholic Mission.
  - Sirasi Kiwuwa (Kitanywa's son): had a daughter called Namala, this was his only child.
- KIBUUKA (Kitanywas' son) had the following children:
  1). Sewagudde also called Mbwanango
  2). Sepiriya Lugeya also called Mulyantungo
  3). Namubiru
  4). Terudiza Nnamubiru omuto
  5). Petero Wakulira,
  6). Kiwuwa (mbwanango was his first child)
  7). Lwatuwabya
  8). Yusuf Kuttakulimuki and
  9). Kakomo

Vunyi the Father

SEMIONI SERUBIRI (Vunyi's son: (his wife was the sister of Nnabigayiri, our step mother and mother of eldest sister in Luyirika's family (Victo Ntabade and Paul Kyaaka, the eldest children for all Luyirika's historical family) This was Vunyi's son. His children all of them died young. He ultimately was burried at Mulago.

•KALITUNSI – KITANYWA (this was the son of Kitanywa), but immigrated to Namutamba in SSingo county (central Uganda). He was a brother to Kiwuwa Siras, a family successor of Kitanywa … their father. Kalitunsi a nick named, was grand father of Katete (deceased) and Kenneth Kiwuwa at Kajjajjansi in Uganda Capital. Siras Kiwuwa was buried at the estate of Kalitunsi and was the first to that cemetery…. Which is wide and extended. Kalitunsi had also another brother, whose name (Kiwanuka) who was raised by the catholic nuns) I Bulemezi county of Cental Uganda. Siras Kiwuwa was the successor to their father Kitanywa. Kenneth Kiwuwa had his three auntie that resided at the Entebbe road. They were daughters of Kibuka who died living at Entebbe. Kibuka was a son of Kalitunsi and were both buried at Nnamutamba in SSingo County of the Kingdom of Buganda in Central of Uganda.

Photo credit by the author.
On the right is Erisha Luyika (my father) and his senior brother (my uncle) Jonathan Musoke Walun'gama

Jonathan Musoke Walun'gama my uncle (father of Gertrude Nakimbugwe, Ezekiel Kiwuwa, and Eldad Kakomo, Nakiboneka, Lukisandasi, and Zulayina Nakibuuka) was the eldest son of the Kitanywa Mikaya Bayise and Kigeya (Lugeya) children that settled at Namakofu, Mityana. Walun'gama was the son of Kigeya the eldest brother to Mikaya Bayise. It will be remembered that, Mikaya Bayise was the father of Erisha Luyirika & Mikayiri Nanfumba (both deceased and rested at Namakofu). Musoke was a self-trained lawyer, though he never went to law school, but practiced and won all his trials. He was briefly a secretary to the high court and attorney general of Buganda kingdom under his Ndiga clan brother Mr. Waswa Kafulu the father of Kizza who owns the Ndiga clan estate. This is the burial ground of the Lwomwa Ndiga clan.

The Children of Yonasani Musoke Walung'ama. (Brother of Erisa Luyirika & Mikayiri Nanfumba and Serubiri):

Zulayina Geneti Nakibuuka ... her mother was Lukiya. Geneti was buried at Namakofu. Her mother was from Bussujju County. She was the only child born to Musoke from Lukiya. It should be remembered that, there was a plan to marry Lukiya, but the plan did not fall well in the care-taker gentleman of Jonathan Musoke. So, the friend of the gentleman, the care taker to Jonathan while visiting the home and semi-palace of this gentleman show Jonathan Musoke methods of communication ability and charm he requestes to marry his daughter, thinking he was a son of the care taker. The care taker agreed and so Jonathan Musoke married Namugambe the daughter of a famous mayor of Kampala. Due to being famous, he gained a lot of land at Mulago which ultimately passed to his daughter Namugambe. In return, on her death, Namugambe gave the pieces of land to her children, Nakimbugwe Meliya Getrida, Lukisandasi Namazi and Ezekiel Kiwuwa Bill. (The two as of writing are now dead.... Bill buried at Namakofu and Nakimbugwe(86 years) with her husband in Bulemezi county.. Bamunanika. Zulayina was never succeeded properly since the successor to her was Jane Nakibuka the daughter of Kyaka Paul the first son of Erisa Luyirika.

Jonathan Musoke at marriage of Namugambe at Kwanjula wedding ceremony in the residence of honourable Sssekiwala (he was king's-kabaka's chief county administrator of Mityana, Uganda) After marriage of Namugambe, Jonathan Musoke Walun'gama, had the following children from Solome Namugambe the daughter of Sekiwala:

Photo provided by friend.

The bako (bridegroom's parents home, home of Mr. Ssekiwala at Mityana, Uganda) receiving gifts and introduction spokesman to the family addressing the crowd of the invited guests to the occasions. 1.Gertulda Meliya Nakimbugwe (the wife of Bulasiyo Kavuma, Kabaka .. kings treasurer) Nakimbugwe was the mother to two famous children, married to famous husbands in Uganda:

i). Mother of MS. Sam Odaka (Margret), ii).Namugambe solome (wife of Dr. Nsibambi, practicing physician in Kampala) Dr. Edward Kiwuwa, the son of Erisa Luyirika, was choosen by her to be the executor and a custodian of her will. In which she stated that if there were to be any conflict in land estate management at namakofu, the professor would be the ultimate final decision maker. And his decision is construed final.

Erinadi Kakomo (would have been the successor to his father Musoke, Jonathan Walun'gama, but inspite of several warnings from his father, he continued to be alcoholic and so his father condemned his behavior and tossed him out from being his successor of him and his estate) Kakomo died and was buried at Namakofu the burial ground of the Jonathan Musoke Walung;ama's family estate. He had two children and was girls.

Puloskovia Nakiboneka whose education was up to 5th grade at Gayaza made her famous in the girls of Uganda. She ended marrying the princess of Toro and had several children with him. But, then later, she divorced him and married a Swedish husband. They stayed at tank hill, Muyenga until the days of bad governments of Amin, the thugs almost killed her and her husband. They wanted to claim all their properties but they survived after several cuts of pangas. Today, she is survived of the children she had from the husband from Toro, since the Swedish husband died without children with her.

Lukisandasi Namazzi was summarily educated at Gayaza. But on one of trips to Nayirobi, Kenya, she met an English man who made her pregnant. He left and disappeared back to Europe with giving chance for Lukisandasi to know him. She raised the child alone. Then, later she met a white man from South Africa who she stayed together for along time and had with him three children. Her child was Veronic, was trained in France

Lukisandasi (1929) as of writing, she is dementia and will be buried in Pittsburgher, Pennyslvania. Her eldest daughter stays in one of the Islands and cut communication with her mother. The last days of Lakisandasi is in the stricted and supervised home of the Nursing home and she is under government supervision with an appointed power of attorney to act for the wishes of her children.

Ezekyeri Kiwuwa, Bill the youngest child in Jonathan Musoke's family. Educated in England in Electricity, but found it difficulty and so opted business where he got a certificate. On coming back to Uganda was protected by a famous father who had famous sisters and famous uncles. They promoted him easily and managed several business enterprises. Married from a famous family. They raised two children together. But they ended up in divorce due to the political instability of Uganda and the insulting language that did not please her father-in law.

His children were: Kiwuwa Musoke and Ian Musoke. Married to white women. Ian the youngest has children but the eldest Jonathan musoke is not. So, worried of losing the family line since the eldest child always is a hair to the father unless has a bad behavior as was in case of Kakomo the elder to Kiwuwa, Musoke.) His children: Ian who has a profession of "human beuty and attire" lives in Minnesota, while the eldest moved to California to stay with his mother. He used to own a caffee while in Minnesota, but now nobody is sure what he does in LosAngeles, CA. He has no child still. Bill Musoke died at age not clear at age of 67 (needs verification). He died from HIV/AIDs a disease virus and a pandemic that inflicted the world from the end of the 20th and actively continued in the 21st century.

Photo credit by the author in legacy to his
older sister and older brother.

Gertrude Nakim bugwe Kavuma – The hero of my life seated with older brother Kyaka, myself, and my niece Nabosa. Ms. Kavuma was the first daughter of my father Jonanthan Walungama-Musoke. She and her husband Brasio Kavuma paid some of my tuition when I was in secondary school at Kako Senior Secondary school in Uganda. My older sister Gertrude looked after me and had promised during my wedding to pay for all drinks alone. She and her husband had me in their home during my vacation, and drove me 200 miles to Masaka to take be back to Kako after vacation. They had a Mercedes Benz and it made the trip feel like only 5 miles. They had two beautiful daughters that I admired of good raising. The eldest was Margret Odaka and the younger was Solome Nsibambi. They were well raised in a good home. I used to stay in a room in their house with the brother of the King of Buganda, Mr. Goloba. Kavuma, her husband, he was the treasurer of the Estate and Finance for the Kingdom of Buganda. This was a highly respectable family in the circles of Africa and the world. And the King of Buganda used to visit them on a constant basis. Gertrude Kavuma was the first daughter of, her parents Solome and Jonathan Musoke Walumgama. And the second was Nakiboneka, and next to her was Eldad Kakomo. The next sister

Lukisandasi Musoke, and Bill Ezekiel Kiwuwa was the youngest child in the family. They had one step sister, Janet Nakibuka and she was the eldest sibling in the family.

Photo provided by brother before his death.

Bill Musoke Kiwuwa at his training in London for electrical engineering and business accounting professional. (Photo provided by older brother before his death.) Omutuba gwa: Katangaza Kikonge (Wanda) Kiwuwa, e Namakofu

REVIEW QUESTIONS

1. What kind of family was the background of the luyirika?
2. Kibonge is called over this family, what role was this character in Luyirika's?
3. What role did Kitanywa play in the Luyirikas?
4. What was the relationship between Yonasani Musoke Walungama and the Luyirika's family?
5. D
6. How does the system of
7. What is stress, and how is it detected?

CHAPTER IV

THE GRANDS & THEIR HERITAGES AND TRICKS FOR SURVIVAL

Bajjajja ffe: Petro Wanda; Gwamba Kitanywa salongo: Gayiya Yakobo Salongo: Mpungu Nnantagya: bano mwe muva (Azala Mulani Serubiri ate azala, tata wa Muhammad Haji Mpungu e Kankolokolo; Balengera, Waswa ne Kato. (Batwerinde of Gomba and succeded by the father of Serubiri of Bugabo on Entebbe road): Balengera, Mpungu Nantajja. Kitanywa, Mpungu Nantajja the father of Mulani Serubiri / Bule)

Petero Wanda Serunkuma: Yazaala Marthias Mayanja ne Yoana Njuba, Tebyasa Mayanja brother of Yoana Njuba and a brother to Erisa Luyirika of Namakofu. Balengera Waswa and Batwerinde Kato of Kyetume (Gomba) were brothers and Kiwuwa (the father of Omukulu serubiri) of Bugabo succeded him); Tebyasa Mayanja was a brother of Yoana Njuba and Martin mayanja (siblings of Kitanywa).

Martia Mayanja – the son of Petro Wanda, Serunkuma, is the father of:

Yazaala abaana bana (4):

Bosa Kyaaka

Chris Sewagude

Kafumbe Polinati, ye yasikira Yoana Njuba, ate yazzala Francis Kinobe, Masaka

Martia Mayanja

Petero serunkuma, ekamwokya

Kyaaka Bosa (Ekatete, Gomba) the son of Martia Mayanja has the following off springs:

Semuyaba Christopher Sewagude
Bone Serunkuma
Nalunkuma
Andrew Kyegombe and
The successor/ hair to Kyaaka Bosa.

Other Kirigendali Mayanja's children are: Vunana the father of :

House Ggwamba and
Nuwa Katete, Musoke
Ntambazi the father of:
- Nasibu Njogeza and
- Mpungu Banadawa, Ali
- Other Kikonge the father of:
- Petro Wanda Katete: yoana Njuba, Albino serunkuma, Marthias mayanja, Albino Serunkuma the father of:
  - Buruno Serunkuma Kibuuka Joseph
  - And Nakimbugwe.... The eldest of them all.

Photo credit by author.

The family was always happy when our parents were around. As you notice above, mother and father are happily seated in their home. Even if there were no electricity, running water, but, it was the center of all of the sixteen children. We always felt safe when we were in the arms of our loving parents. Father used to sit in the chair and began singing: Bwendirab abafa mu kristo nga bazukira... baliwebwa ekitibwa kya katonda... meaning: If father were to see those who died in the name of Jesus resurrected, will be given the glory of God ... He sang this song always with a smile of hope. (The religion circulated in all of his body)

As mentioned above of the background of this gentleman, Luyirika died a stout advocacy of seventh Day Adventist beliefs in Uganda and one of the pioneers of this church in Uganda. He worked with missionaries and moved in errands that covered the state of Uganda as teacher and evangelist and outstanding pastor (preacherof his time).

Nabigayiri Nakkazi: She was his first wife and had with her two children:

1. Victo Ntabadde born (6- 20-1928)

Victo Ntabade the eldest child (daughter of Erisa Luyirika). She independently and under the protest of her father, when she turned of matures age she married a husband of Moslem faith and had several children with him. They are: names to check; then she married two more husbands and had children to each one. (Names to be checked)

Victo Ntabade resides at Kasubi the out skirt of Kampala, capital of Uganda. She is a wonderful model to her children. They are all loving and close to each other inspite of the different fathers. By the time, her father Erisa Luyirika passed away in 1988, she had been reconverted to the SDA belief of believers. She is a stout SDA as was her father when he passed away. Victo Ntabade, she is also known as Namukasa. This was a name given to her by her mother and her uncles since she stayed with them after her mother left Luyirika. There was a child that lost during pregnancy.

The mother of Paul Kyaka and Victo Ntabade was Nabbigayiri Nakkazi that resided at Namutamba. Nabbigayiri was the sister of the wife of serubiri the brother of Luyirika. Luyirika met Nabbigayiri in the home of Serubiri. The parents of Luyirika admornished he from a continued marriage to Nabbigayiri's mother was of Ndiga clan. It was also assumed that Serubiri his wife was Susan Mbawade, Samali Lwandeka was their mother and their father was Mukaya living in Mukibuto village near Bakijjulula; to lose all his children was due to the same reason. He had several children but they all died before adult age, their mother was of Mamba clan, Paul Kyaka Mukasa resembles our grandfather of the entire estate of Luyirika Kitanywa.

Paul is pictured with his (our) cousin brother
in the white shirt at his estate.

2. Paul Kyaka Mukasa (11-23-1931): ***

He is the senior brother to the auther of the days of our lives. He is standing with his uncle-in law. In his home.

Self named himself Mukasa due to his mother and uncles as they were with their under the supervision of their mother when she left their father.

Serina Nanzigu (Nalongo): the mother of 14 children.

** (father & mother) in their local home and neighborhoods. The attire they had represented the typical Baganda's tradition of home and living life style. It is Besweri Bakisula, who took her away on bicycle in the evening to Luyirika's home. There were no introduction ceremonies. The baby Zawedde Nakiboneka, was due while her mother was in her father's home, that's why they would not wait for her to be born, but to deliver the mother to the father of the baby to avoid (rituals in the home), Mawunikirano in Luganda Language.

There was never a weeding to this young lady who was married in traditional marriage. She was brought on bicycle by her brother Bakisula Besweri. She was brought to the home of Erisa Luyirika at night when she was four months pregnant to her first child daughter... Zawedde. ..... There had never been a church weeding for thse couples. They stayed together until Nalongo Serina Nanzigu left Luyirika in this world in 1986. She died of stroke based from the worries of losing her eldest children... starting with Zawedde,

Waswa, Kato, and then Kizza in addition to the youngest who preceeded all of them. She had a lot of stress in her latest life due to the death of her eldest children.

Fenekansi was the brother of Serina Nalongo who lived with her.

3. Zawede Nakiboneka. The first child of Nalongo Nanzigu (12-11-1934) she died from complications of pregnancy and abortion that was due to some swallowing traditional medicinal. She died at 3:00 a.m. She had been sent by her parents to her uncle bakisula after they had noticed that she was pregnant to the brother of neighbor "sawa" a rich neighbor and very influential on the village. The parents did not want to influence their children and being the pastor of the church in the neighborhood/ on the village. The brother of Sawa though did not come out clearly, did influence displeasure to his brother Sawa who passed his feelings to his wife that was good friend of the mother of Zawede. Zawede died at the home of his uncle at Mutundwe and was buried there also. Zawede was succeded by her young sister Edith Nabigujju (buried) at Namakofu. She died without a child. She died in 1954. Eriya Waswa and Erisa Kato ... (tweens 9-19-1936) Waswa was born first and then Kato followed.

Eriya waswa was named Luyirika, and Erisa Kato was named Katete. They both were raised in a true Christian faith of Seventh day Adventist. They both were headmasters of out standing primary schools.

Waswa was headmaster of Nabagereka primary school and Katwe parents school both in the center of Kampla the capital of Uganda.

ERISA Kato Katete trained at kibuli TTC was posted to several schools ie. In Entebe primary school where he snatched his former wife though did not last long. Then was a headmaster at Kanyange primary school, Kyalugondo primary school and kikyusa primary school.

The children of Eriya Waswa Luyirika (died in 1966 from cancer of head):

Lusi Namuga was his wife and got her from a Muslim family. The father objected to Waswa to have his daughter pregnant, but it was too late to change and waswa was such an educated and influential civic leader and so he gave in as long as Waswa was willing to take her as his wife. Which he did and so the family life began. Milliam Nakimbugwe Gertruda; Born at Mulago hospital in November 2nd, 1963

Edward Luyirika (1964) (3 children)
William Kakomo (1966) (11 children)
Edith Nabosa Najja….. (dec. 1967) (2 children)
The children of Paul Kyaaka Mukasa (Elder to the tweens) 15 children
Jane Nakibuka 1956 (son in London)
Night Nabitula _ (1958)
Pross Nakiboneka – (1960)
These were children of Namudu as their mother.
(Kiwuwa Robert –1960)
Robert Kiwuwa was the eldest son of Kyaaka, Paul, Mukasa, and Luyirika. He was his lovely son. When he left him and went in London, he met a Musoga girl who had been exposed to HIV/AIDS. She died from it and so did Robert. Above you are looking at Robert being cared for by the social worker of the metropolitan community / the city health department. Robert Kiwuwa at his last days being cared for and assisted by social worker in East London. UK.

5. Kinobe Daniel 1962 also died from HIV/AIDS.
These two their mother was Mirianm Nambassa.
Other children are:
Victo Ntabade
Daniel Katete 1978
Ellen Mpungu 1977 (mother Sarah
Ddina Nakimbugwe (1978)
The same mother of the two above. Three more children the names were not given as the father was clarifying some issues as of writing this book. Back to the birth of the twins;

Erisa Kato pictured above.

Eriya Waswa pictured above twin brother to Erisa Kato and died in 1967.

THE BIRTH OF MY TWIN BROTHERS --- ERISA KATO- KATETE AND ERIYA WASWA AND RELATED TRADITIONS OF THE TWINS.

The birth of these twin brothers in my family changed the morphology of my home. In Africa, the birth of a twin, is a symbol of great parents. Several traditions are usually done to the twins. Grandparents and family relatives tend to celebrate the birth of the twins. There are several activities that call for the public to pay attention to the Baganda traditions, beliefs and culture. Usually drums sound in the streets and community participation has an automatic invitation to join in. The mother of the twins does not meet face to face with her mother in law. The mother of the twins hides her face from the public and is objected to meet her in laws with uncovered face and eyes. There is a character of foods that has got be served and that special dishes are to be served to the newly born twin parents. Names of the twins are by tradition known by everyone in Uganda and so are the parents. In this instances, the first birth of the twins is called "Waswa" and the next if is a boy, is called "Kato". If they were girl twins, their names are clearly known to the public. The first girl is usually named: "Babirye and the sister is usually "Nakato."

The parent's role and their names are transformed automatically to new names. The new Mother is called "Nalongo" and the new father is called "Salongo." These two names distinguish the new parents from the rest of parent group. It is a great honor to have those names in the Kiganda family. As parents, you receive a great honor in the society and you are on public functions elevated to high proud and always consulted in matters of community crisis. The society gives you the position of a wise society leader that deserves to be consulted in case of community needs.

Marriage of the Twins

Twins have special marriage opportunities according to their birth rights. Since "Waswa" is usually the eldest, has to marry first and the parents have to recognize the weeding as such. The death and funeral of one of the twins, means, that, the surviving child cannot attend the other's funeral rites. It has to be kept secret so as not to destruct the surviving twin.

In a family of mine, Waswa the first born of the twins. He was energetic and had leadership skills of the family. He married earlier and had that privilege to have the first birth of their children amongst the twin brothers. Kato, the young twin brother, was not invited to the occasion of the funeral of the death of his twin brother Eriya Waswa. On the other hand, Kato's marriage was well received since at that time, Waswa was still arriving. It was a great occasions for these two siblings. Waswa did not have a church bell marriage. But, instead, had a traditional marriage. By traditional marriage, the bride introduces her fiancé' to the parents. There then, gifts and money come to the couple from all directions. The wealthier and richer the side of the brides 'groom family, the more gifts including cows, goats, chicken and various clothes are provided to the parents of the brides. This was the only occasion in which Waswa participated into. As mentioned that, since the bride was expecting a child, and the parents of the bride were not of the same religion of the bridegroom, it was inevitable to end their happiness of marriage with local tradition. But, for Kato, it was the opposite. He got engaged to one of his students and quickly traditional ceremony and church bell were organized and it formed a reunion of the marriage in the church.

Kato's' weeding was so colorful, and so did all the joy of expected marriage from young couples. But, it did not meet that expectation. It was a rock marriage. This joy of married couple, did not result into children. Medical tests were done, but the bride could not have children. Kato, however, had to move in to a single woman in the neighborhood who ultimately had two children for him. Had he not to do that, Kato would have never had a child since he had married a girl that could not have children.

On the other hand, his brother Waswa, before he died in March 1964 had four children. But, Kato, his wife by the name Margret introduced to him by the church members at Entebbe church in Central Uganda. She was Margret and both her brothers and sisters were from Kiwafu village in Entebbe. They were legally married at

Najjanankumbi church of SDA and their honey moon was spent in the home of his elder brother Paul Kyaka Mukasa.

Kato had two wives. One was not legally married, but she had children from her. But, on the other he married her in the church, but had no children. Margret his legal marriage left him and he struggled all the time for along time to bring her home, but she dodged him all the time. When she openly told him that the medical examination had revealed that she could not bear him a child, Kato was confused. Finally, in the absence of a woman in his life, Kato settled with a single neighborly lady whose home was close to the school where he was teaching.

Abisagi: This lady that lived at Kyalugondo in central part of Buganda was born and raised Uganda. She was a brown complex, tall lady. She had an infectious smile for she was so nice and kind. No wonder why Kato had to favor in her. For even Kato was no different from her. Since both were exciting to stay with, it indeed made sense to have beautiful children as it turned out to be. No body can accuse Kato to have children out of wedlock. For Kato was alone for a long time since his wife had abandoned him and was no where to be found in the home except that of her parents in Entebbe. Kato did no wrong to have a family with this lady. Of course she had children with another man, but the time Kato had a child with this lady, the man was already in prison for civil cases. The woman advised Kato that she was alone and had not been married to any one tha, even the man she had had children with; she had no marriage with him, but instead habitation. However in community property law of traditional marriage in Uganda, they could qualify to be married. Kato's children (3):

Erisa Katete: Ono wa kato asoka era yali musajja naye teyafuna mukisa kugenda wala musomero. Ba tata be abato bagezako okumuyamba naye nga nabo tebesobola bulungi nadala bweyali akyasula Entebe. Naye byagana okuyitamu obulungi. Oluvanyuma yasabibwa okukuma enyumba ya professor Kiwuwa ekansanga, Ekampala. Kyoka era ate yanyakula sente za tatawe omuto nga azigya kubapangisa. Naduka yeka awaka nava ekansanga nga kitawe omuto tanamuzula. Newankubade oluvanyuma yawandika ebaluwa eyokwenenya nga tanafa ndwade eriwo kakati eya silimu.

Photo provided by friend.

Katete and his companion at Kwanjula ceremony at Gaba near Kasanga in Uganda. Katete picture second from right was accompanying his friend to the occasion of introduction (okwanjula) near his former residence at Gaba. His former residence was the home of his uncle Professor Kiwuwa- Khiwa at Kansanga. He was the replacement when his uncle was away studyin in USA. He was wearing a white gown in a company of his other friends who were joining to a ceremony of their friend. In Uganda, it is a custom to wear this attire if you seek to be introduced by your fiancé before her parents. If you were the centrally, you may easily miss the wife. Traditionally you have to be humble and someone else speaks for you. You do not utter any single word during the occasion. It is a sign of respect and humility to the parents of the girl. Also, on the same occasion, both sides have to select a spokesman for either side in order to be welcomed in the occasion of the home. So, Katete was on this occasion and seemed to enjoy himself and his colleagues the day of the introduction at Gaba introduction ceremony for his friend's family and fiancé.

WHAT MY FATHER TOLD ME AT THREE IN THE MORNING

Photo provided by my brother, Walungama Iddi.
GRAND FATHER; Amulani Serubiri

The great man of his time, made the county of Butambala (central part of Uganda) to be known in many parts of Uganda. He was smart and intelligent. When the Butambala County was awarded to the Moslem religious faith to appease the King of Buganda, for Mpungu being a strong fighter on behalf of the King and won the war. He devised methods of him and his family to survive. He was a parent to several children, notably Mpungu, who he moved with and in addition with his other brother Batulumayo Kiwuwa, and ran and hid at the home of their twin brother Kato Batwerinde the twin brother of Waswa Balengera. Batwerinde, Kato, and Yakobo Waswa Balengera (Bugabo resident near Entebbe international airport in Central Uganda).

Batwerinde allowed staying with them for a while. Meantime, that time was intended to cool off the struggle of Moslem to the power struggle that had been awarded by the King of Buganda (Central Uganda) Mr. Amulani, however, could not stay with his brother, but decided to move with his brother Waswa Yakobo Balengera and moved with him for a while and decided to settle at Bugonzi on Masaka Road. At Bugonzi, joined his brother Ernest Kiwuwa who lived with his sister Polina. Both children belonged to our grandfather Kitanwya. Our grandfather Mulani serubiri, decided to constantly communicate with his former half brother Banadawa, Mpungu. One day, he felt sick, died and was buried at Bule village at Butambala in the vicinity of the homestead of the mile that used to belong to the ownership of the Katangaza Mutuba, which when its leader was deposed due to the insurgents of Islamic revolution, Banadawa, Mpungu took over the land. But, he had convinced the elders that since Kyaaka was no longer alive, for he had a heart attack! Mpungu Banadawa, moved from his former resident of Kyenajjanja (near Blue) and had his new home at Bule.Banadawa Mpungu was a furious warrior that could not allow non Moslem to stay in awarded county! His brother the county chief lived a twenty miles apart, and so he instructed that a non-Islam would not reside in that county unless had been circumcised. A lot of Christians including the grand fathers of this author (Kitanwya with his son Mikaya Bayise).

They created new homes outside Butambala County. Kitanywa had several children ie. Siras Kiwuwa, Nakatude, Nakimbugwe, Mikaya Bayise, Kigeya, he had them at Mpanga, in Mityana, central part of Uganda. When, Kitanwa had another deal at Ndejje, he moved there but, he had left his favorite son Siras Kiwuwa at the Mpanga village. Also, when Kitanwya their father died, Siras Kiwuwa was his successor. Siras Kiwuwa, resided in his father's home. When Siras Kiwuwa fell sick, he was taken to his other brother Kalitunsi who had moved to stay at Namutamba, and was buried there. His sister Nakimbugwe when she died after divorce with Mr. Mbwasiri a head administrator at Bugabo, village, she was buried at Namunyanyula near Namutamba where she had got a home for herself.

Finally, Serubiri Mulani with his leadership, he saved a land for his brother Bernadicto Kiwuwa, and his daughter, Polina. When Benedict Kiwuwa died, he left the land to his sister Polina. Finally, when Polina died, the land was taken over by Mr. Mpungu, the father of Idd Walungama and the current prime minister of Katangaza sub-clan being led by Professor Edward Kiwuwa, the grandson of both Serubiri Mulani and kigeya Bayise.

In other words, our grandfather Serubiri Mulani is attributed for his uniqueness to save the family of Kitanywa and his father Kikonge the great father of all being mentioned above. Serubiri Mulani died when he was 84, and his son Mpungu at Masaka was 87 and Kitanywa was 108, and Siras Kiwuwa was 87, and Lugeya who had a child in his half sister Nakatude died when he was 86 and Balengera died when he was 102, and his brother kato Batwelinde was 87, and Banadawa Mpungu was 83 (died in 1937), and Siras Kiwuwa was 83, Yonasani Musoke was Walungama was 86 and Erisa Luyirika was 84 and Petero Alina the daughter of Balengera died when she was 106, and the two surviving sisters of Mustafa Lugeya, buried at Seta and died of ages 102 and 101. They were both Moslems. So, Mr. Mulani goes in history of the family as one of the greatest protector of the family and was a link of both Moslem and non-Moslem converted families.

Understanding the family of Twin Brothers: Erisa Kato & Eriya Waswa (Salongo and Nalongo Luyirika's children) <u>The children of the offspring are of Kato:</u>

<u>Kato had two children from his maiden neighborhood. Katete and Kagere.</u>

Kato Katete and his children were:

Edward Kiwuwa the surviving grandson of Erisa Kato one of the twins was born in his grand fathers' home Professor Edward Kiwuwa, which he was asked as housekeeping at Kansanga, Uganda surburbs of Uganda. (2) Victo Nanzigu is one of the eldest grand children in the family of Erisa Luyirka the grandfather of the Kato Katete and robina Kagere. She is now a practicing registered nurse in the central parts of Uganda. * <u>Robinah Kagere Ntabade:</u>

Photo credit by author.

Robin's father: Erisa Kato twin brother to
Eriya Waswa and died in 1971.

Robina Kagere was a favorite child to Kato. Her mother was pregnant when Kato her father died in an Automobile accident. As you notice her, she was well educated and completed all nursing school programs in Uganda. She was elevated to administration of several clinics in Uganda. She is an excellent nurse and well respected in the entire Uganda. With her uncle Professor Khiwa, kiwuwa on her side, she paraises Lord that she came out to be an outstanding professional nurse. The family is very proud of her.

John Mpungu Kizza (Lubega): This gentleman used to use the name of Mr. Lubega his half brother. He also used his credentials to be awarded business certificates and also to be promoted as business representative for Mubende chamber of Commerce. His death was controversial being that, there were a few colleagues of his that he worked with that did not like him to move over them. Although it was officially recorded to have died from yellow fever, but still all his wealth was swindled by his friends that did not like him to move away from them and be promoted to prominence over them. (Kiza had ten (10) children when he died. He was smart and very intelligent and visionary thinker. He survived on his own while holding his family alone. He crafted his bother his achievements through the success of his brother Lubega. Kizza had several wives and died when he had the following children: The following children had the same Mother (by the name: Naluyima):

1). Chrisitna – Nasereka was his first child in his first wife of youth.
2). Margret Ntabade, died and buried at e Namakofu.
3). Namirembe Harriet. (She was buried at Namakofu.) His second wife: Teopista who had two children for him and they are: Kakomo Kizza who had four children when he died, and Kiwanuka when he died had two (2) children.
4). Kakomo ... (4) children
5). Kiwanuka he died but left two children and they are all at Mubende. Kizza had several other children. They were born by his legal married wife by names: Teddie Namboze who now resides at Busale with her current husband "Balihagira". The following children are in line to the birth from this mother:
6). Grace Nakimbugwe (has 6 children, but were booted out of her husbands' family when her husband died.
7). William Nanfumba Kigongo (3)
8). Eseza Nabigujju
9). Luci Nakato (deceased)
10). Norah Kizza Kiwuwa Nampungu (She is married to Mr. Bosa Mugoya, and now a mayor of Mubende town council as its city planner)
11). Ruth Nakatete, Najja —— was born on November 1977 (not married yet)

Joshua Kigeya Kamya (1940)

This highly learned gentlenma was noted to be knowlegiable of the world due to his achieved accolades. He was trained at Katikamu for primary education, then Bugema. He had misfortune at Bugema and while there it was decided in the interest of Bugema SDA School and Mr. Kigeya to move on another school where he competed aggressively. He moved to Lubiri Secondary school. He passed and was supposed to move on other high academic ladders. Instead, after teaching at Najjanankumbi SDA School, he scored a scholarship to study in Tananarive, Madagscar in the Indian Ocean. Since these were time of turbulence, when he went back for vacation in Uganda, he was denied a visa to come back to Madagascar. He worked in Uganda until he scored another grant from Nnajjanankumbi Seventh day foundation program with assistance of Dr. Kiseka, Kasato and Buule. Etc. He went to study in the Spicer Memorial College, Ganshkind, India. After completing 4 years with BS he continued and attained a masters' degree in history. He came back and started teaching in Uganda until he got admitted to complete a terminal degree in Andrews University in Michigan in US. After arrivasl in US with ofcourse some help from his brother Dr. Kiwuwa. The overall, of coming to US was done by himself handdly. Then, he brought over his family and there started a new life in US. He got a master's and Ph.D at different Universities especially University of Wisconsin where he got a Ph.D This gentleman is the leader and successor of Luyirika and Luyirika estate every where around the world especially at Namakofu, Mityana, Uganda.

The family of Dr. Joshua Kigeya is well off than some few members of Luyirika line. The gentleman is well off. He has estates in Uganda, and USA. He lives in Kalina. Very well off than any other mentioned above in the family. Joshua Kigeya Kamya's family blessings: (he has 5 grands), please, verify the facts. His wife is Abisagi Nayiga. Parents of Ms. Abisagi Nayigga live in Bulemezi county & Bululi county in central part of Buganda/Uganda. Children are: 1). Jonathan Musoke (3)… (1-1- 1977) 2).Daniel Kigeya (2). (12-3-1978)3).Grace Zawedde Kigeya4).Gideon Kiterera Kigeya Daniel Kigeya is a graduate with a masters or working towards it. He is a professional advisor in the University at the State of Wisconsin in USA. All children ie. Jonathan Musoke, Daniel Kigeya and Grace, all reside in Wisconsin; yet ****Gideon Kiterera the youngest of all is set to continue his education in the homeland of his parents, Uganda. (Here Gideon is beginning a comfortable life with his parents. He was a baby of a few weeks old. Joseph Kaggwa Serubiri (1941) (died in May 2014) This gentleman used to reside in Mubende (Western part of Uganda). This gentleman has resembled a like the stature of their father in the days of his age. He did not go too far in school, but learnt and worked as electrician in Uganda. That did not stay for along time. He turned to be a welding by profession. He has had several choices of ladies that gave him several children: He has (9) children although a few have passed away due to HIV/AIDS disease. He has 15 grands. 1).Joseph Sewagude (4)2).John Kitanywa (5) died from HIV/AIDs3).Paul Katete, died when he was 13 and was buried at Namakofu. But did not die from HIV/AIDS. The above children were born from his former wife a half cast. She passed away in October 1981. Again, this gentleman is recorded to be a father of the following children: 4).William Kafumbe (1). The mother of this son was a Mutoro (from Toro district). She died and so the uncles brought the son to the father. He is well established in Uganda armed forces. 5).Teopista Namazzi (5) children. She is suffering from HIV/AIDS diseases. But uses the latest therapeutic treatment therapies.

6).Joseph Luyirika ... this was brought to him by his mother when the son demanded it. He is growing a responsible man, but with no formal education. 7).Kagwa Luyirika. This man is relatively very young and was brought recently in his life by his mother.

EDWARD KHIWA KIWUWA

A highly well established and learned pioneer in Luyirika family to climb to the pyramid of academic ladders with a terminal degree... the Ph.D. In his photo, when he lasted many years in studies abroad, he went back home and found his parents dead. The photo was taken on the day his mother died while at his brothers' home Professor Erisa Semakula in Colorado, USA. These were mountains of Colorado where he and his brother had gone to reduce tensions of the death of his mother, Nalongo Luyirika, Nanzigu.

The second photo is when the author was a student in Moscow University and this was a winter semester. He had held in his right arm the bag of textbooks. He was tired and walking in midst of winter. As a foreigner you had to be well confined in heavy warm clothes given to you at the beginning and arrival in Moscow. You had to wear 8 pieces on you, otherwise the police would give you a ticket for abusing the state law. The State of Ukrain was also a memory to this young man. On arrival when he and other citizens and residents in Ukraine had to travel by train. Here the author travelled for three days on train. The funy part of this trip, is that, when we came close to leave the boarder of the Russian Republics and heading to Ukrain, the Militia stopped all travelers and moved out everybody and we walked a half kilometer necked and had a real good shower. Of course women went a different direction and men went another direction to have a hot tab. It was unusual to me, because I had never done it before. But, I was assured that it was normal in Soviet Union at that time to share life as one body and that was a part of Lennin's teaching. Of course, we gave our clothes to store man who kept them for us until we completed the shower and came back in the train. We were told at last on the way, that it was the Ukrainian culture to be together as you discover each one's life. Well, it was a challenge to the young man.

TIMOTHY BAYISE (2)

Timothy Bayise had three children from his wife, but one of their boys died soon. He did not have too long to live. He was a young man, but could not complete high school. The family was very upset of the events leading to his death. The remaining boy and a girl Dinah have grown and completed the college. They are well respected citizens of Uganda.

Photo credit by author.

This gentleman is a professional carpenter. Although, he does a lot of self made jobs/ occupations, he has been on his own with barely no one supporting him in life. It has not been easy during some parts of his life. During the government of IDI Amin, he almost lost his life due to the jealousy of his peer colleagues in the timber/ carpentry work shop. He was imprisoned at Luzira high prison for no basis at all. Although the family and colleagues, friends and family members, his brother in America with the help of Ruth Sebiranda and her father Katamba, who was then the permanent secretary in the ministry of internal affairs, helped me to move him out of the high prison. He found out that the reasons were of jealousy from co-workers and so helped me and released him on the assumption that, I would look after him. That way, God spared him for the family. The next morning when I called the permanent secretary he went directly to Luzira and released him. Ofcourse, I was planning to marry his daughter Ruth Nnabiranda. Of course the plan did not go through due to being and staying overseaes. Another person that was living in Uganda took over and there the plan ended. I could not have a visa and yet his parents wanted to see me before they could release their daughter.

Bayise's family: 1).Yakob James Balengera… was born October 7, 1980 This young man is extremely bright. He completed a B.A from Makerere University in Social Sciences. He is planning to continue on for masters'. 2).Job Luyirika (Died of a sudden death and caused a great disappointment to this family. The 3).Loyi Dinna Namazzi … a potential graduate from Makerere/ Bugema University. She too has a bright future. Loyi the youngest daughter to this family was born in 1984.

EDISA NABIGUJJU (2)

Edisa passed away in 1995 of heart pressure. She played a big role in providing physical therapy to their mother (Luyirika)'s. She definitely was under depression to care for both of her parents until they passed away in her eyes. Edisa, had a failed marriage. Before she died she had two children in different fathers: 1).Katie … was married but her husband died of HIV/AIDS. She is a tween mother. (Remember she is not a member of Ndiga clan) 2).Nerima … very bright girl. She scored to join the University with one of the highest point on the advanced level in Uganda. She is even, still leading them/ fellow student's st the University. Her father was trained physician and a Musoga by tribe.

BESWERI VUNYI LUMINSA

(4) He is a graduate of a famous University of seventh day Adventist in Uganda… the Bugema (SDA). He holds a BA, but has had difficulty to utilize it economically due to the iniquities that

surround his past. He is struggling that, may be as Job regained favor from God so will be Luminsa. Luminsa's Children (off springs): His formal wife of marriage was: Sarah Margret Nambajje Birabwa. 1).Moses Kafumbe... March 8, 19832).Esetha Namirembe, May 9, 19843).Babirye ne Nakato This family has gone through trials and tribulations and it was God's mercy that is preserving this family to safety. The man hates the wife and so does the wife. As a result, the family is broken up in family partition. Some children belong to the father and other to the mother. However, since he was lucky that his oldest brothers gave him financial support, he completed the degree and if he stays on course he will redeem himself. But, he has to accept that, their marriage is over. He should live his former wife alone and the former wife do the same? But should be communicating for the goodness of their children.

ANNA NAMALA (8) children: She is a girl in the family and so her children are not easily accessible for recording.

KIKONGE (Nkonge), ENOCH: He claims when he is sober that he has 2 children but they are all under his wife's custody. However, the family is not conviced until they talk to child and there own will confirm.

MANYA BIGAMBO, DEBORAH.

This girl was raised with a relaxed environment by her parents. She is the last born to the deceased family of Erisa Luyirika. She jokingly did not go to school and as a result, she did not achieve surviving skills. She currently resides with her uncles and grands on the side of her mother. She had her first child from a congole's peasant working for the family. He left her with the baby to rise and went in hiding up to now the child doe not know his father. The boy is well known in football divisions of Uganda. He is a boy. The other children are married and adults.

DR. EDWARD KHIWA-KIWUWA (DR)

The background for this page is under review and soon will be re-written to educate about others this man. His influence in the world is such surmountable that the page has a lot of variable information for others to learn. Professor Edward Khiwa- Kiwuwa the author; "WHAT MY FATHER TOLD ME AT THREE IN THE MORNING: MEMORIES OF OUR LIVES........."

MIKAYIRI NANFUMBA (brother to Luyirika)

This man who was an alcoholic during his final days, he gave a hard time to mother of the Luyirika family. He had no wife and as such, the child-daughter he had was from that of fellow Ndiga clan his name was Serunkuma. Through Serunkuma's wife, he had a baby and named her "Nakityo" (she has 10) children, but not in good terms with children of Luyirika estate. However, things may change tomorrow.

(Left) Mikayiri Nanfumba was one of the brother of Erisa and the author of <u>The Document: What My Father Told Me at Three in the Morning.</u> He was a leader who coordinated and assisted the British to galvanize the people of Uganda to go to war and fight against East Asia. He became the commander of the people.

(Right) Serubiri was a courageous hero who fought side by side with the English people from England in the Second World War. They fought in Bruni under the English colonial leadership. When he came back, he was recognized as a hero in his home country. He is one of the grandfathers of Salongo Erisa.

Mikayiri Nanfumba; the young brother of Erisa Luyirika

These two men were; one on the right, were the parents of Salongo Erisa the father of the author of <u>The Document: What my Father Told Me at Three in the Morning.</u> The administrative organs of Mpungu Clan: (11) Each organ is having its own district in which it falls under, that, its decision is final, known in vernacular as "Mituba": Nanfumba – HQ. Kasekere (Bweya)/ Butambala county in Uganda

Kayemba – HQ. Ssaka --- Bweya
Nakatampewo – Bulugu (Bweya)
Kakomo … Bweya
Katangaza Banadawa – Bule (Butambala)
Lwasamitala …. Kasansala
Luyirika --- Kyenajjanja (butambala0
Katete – eBuulwe, Butambala
Tekana- eneganagana (Mirembe)
Katangaza –Kikonge – Namakofu (Mityana)
Semugonde – Kayinge, Butambala.

REVIEW QUESTIONS

1. Outline the live and progress of Luyirika?
2. What made the family happy for around the clock?
3. What role do Welly the eldest one usually play after the death of the family? Describe
4. Who of the two families have more children, how ol

CHAPTER V

THE ORGIN OF DR. EDWARD KHIWA – KIWUWA'S GRAND PARENTS AND THEIR LINE OF AUTHORITY

IN THE SOCIETY OF UGANDA AND AFRICA.

Photo credit by author.

KATETE

A.	B.
Kikonge (Nkonge) (brothers)	Kirigendali (Mayanja)
Kitanywa*Balengera**Katula *Kiwuwa	Nntambazi*
*Bayise & Kigeya*Lugeya & Tebyasa *katula	*Njogeza*. Dawa
Luyirika Yonasni *Seyiga * Sewagude* katula*	Nasibu * Saad K
J.Kigeya * Bill K * * * Kibuka	* Sekawu/segwa* Abb
* * * *	*

Remember the line of controlling the Emituba is very strong and lengthy. More is pending to this historical family book. Please, report the children born to each Luyirika's heritage and reminants.

Kikonge: Kiwuwa Mayanja Kirigendali
Kitanywa/ Balengera Musoke Ntambazi
Mikaya Bayise/ Mustafa Lugeya Banadawa Ali Mpungu/Njoge
Luyirika Ssalongo/ The two oldest saad Kafumbe / segwanyi
Josua Kigeya / Kiwuwa Abby kafumbe / segwanyi mpungu
To be owomutuba;

You should own a piece of land / or a permanent address where your domains / clienteles have to meet with you at any time.

Must have an academic of a 12th grade to understand and converse in a language that is well versed by all Ugandans and be able to represent your constituency in case of any challenge or misunderstanding with members of public that do not speak Luganda.

Be able to be a good citizen where respect is demanded by your district.

Avoid embarrassment of the clan & Omutuba members you represent.

You can be appointed to the rank at any age.

Seeks to be influential to the society.

Should be of a sound mind to be able to make decisions for the district.

* Three fourths (3/4) of the home families you lead (empya ze nju yobwajjaja can drop you and select a new leader who can bring stability. But the owolunyiriri has to approve in addition to the omukulu we ssiga. To be Owolunyiriri: You should meet all criterions mentioned in the above for Omutuba..... (A, B, C, D)

You should be able to recite a minimum of five (5) grandparents in succession as hereditary line.

Be able to settle conflicts in your line.

Should be the leader of the clan for that district, but stands in as an advisor, should be wealth (able to sustain his living & family) D.when turn to be feeble, an immediate person with the conditions above should be chosen (¾ of the family of each line of the grand parents can vote you out.) it should be noted that, owolunyiriri must lead (6) six lines with whom all families must end up with one grand-grand parent (the last to be remembered by that group) Owolugya: Is chosen by the owner of that lugya (home), or elders compromise with the children/ and other descendants.

Must maintain that home inherited/ and others of his family's home.

He cannot sell tha land/ home when beneficiaries to cater for are still around regardless the differences in the background of each beneficiary.

Could be of any age

Must be sober much of the time

That power could be removed but the land/home cannot be taken away. (The temporary leader of the beneficiaries & elders could vote on the action.)

Owessiga: A person with sound mind can be without considering hereditary benefits

The elders of all Emituba (select) and with a majority vote, becomes owessiga.

The majority in the Mituba group could vote you out, but with the approval of the owakasolya (omukulu wekika.

Must meet the requirements of the residency

Ssentebe we Mituba mu ssiga: Must be well established

Must be a respectable adult

Must be educated to above 12th, grade

Must be able to listen and help to resolve changes.

Must be sober and be able to work with Katikiro (prime minister) and other mituba.

Could be advised to move out of the office if he cannot assist in the annual get together programs.

THE VALLEY OF TEARS (BURIAL GROUND) OF THE LOVED ONES

Not far away from the home of the family at Namakofu, is the burial ground of these pro-founded leaders mentioned above. The area is widely grown with death of Luyirika's family. First was, his father. Michael Bayise, who died an old age, lived many years. He was born in (1830 – 1945). He was a flamboyant man during his teenage & youthful life. He was a well known King's subject in the days when King of Buganda was the most visible empire during colonial period to the continent of Africa. The death in this small valley is based on the love left for each living before death.

Yes, here is my feeling about the two: I admired the love and cherished my father and mother. Something that lasted for fifty golden years, the 50th year being the year of my father's demise. I often told myself that theirs was the kind of marriage I fervently pray have simple, sincere, lasting, and abounding in love, courage and understanding. The day my daddy died, my heart broke, not only for my own grief, but for the grief of seeing such a blessed marriage come to a sudden end right before the eyes of my siblings and nephew and nieces. That closed the chapter of the love of parents; since mother had preceded his death and had been laid in the valley of tears as well.

And how will it be the people who have lost not only fathers, mothers, children, life time partners who open their lives through thick and thin, who dream together and journeyed together and found meaning in each other's lives?

How are to begin grieving for them? Where could we ever find the tears to weep, tears that will pour out and cry in behalf of our torn and shattered hearts?

In the valley of tears, lie several remnants of the family. The valley has tombs of the clever, smart, scholars, administrators, managers, business men and Women, and the famous and un-known. The valley also harbors glories of the achievers and the disappointed in life. The beautiful flowers surrounding the valley and the green banana plants and the tall sugar plantains are great memories of those who planted them and left and buried in the same valley vegetation. Yes, it is the home of the old that died over five hundred years ago, and young that has lived in the valley with short time.

STRESS REDUCTION

If stress had a sound, it would be that of a buzz saw reaping into shop metal. The business community loses $100 billion annually because of stress estimates Donald T. Decarlo, senior vice president of commercial insurance Resources. If you take into account decreased worker efficiency, sick days, and workers compensation paid out because of stress, there are some experts who think the estimate may be on low side. As the information of age intensifies, we can expect to be dealing with more stimuli at an accelerated rate in the future. This means more stress. The twenty first century has moved in with internet and technology age, means more communication improved, jobs eliminated and replaced with modern technology. Seeking employment, is meant to compete with what technology can offer the employer, and until the services of technology are readily available, more stress will be on rise and competition for expertise, will continue. If you know how to relieve stress, your down-time can be minimized.

The reason bad stress often goes undetected is that the cause goes undetected. Even if you do notice what's bothering you, you probably don't realize that the tension from stress hangs around long after the cause is gone. To use an analogy, consider an evening day of both bride and brides groom what they go through when tomorrow is the weeding. Preparations and rehearsals, lack of appetite, and looking perils sometime, is due to the moment of excitement which is due to come. Once the act is done and over, what you have got a sustained tension. Likewise, you may initially get over wound by a problem. But once the problem seems to be rectified you may still be stuck at highest level of excitement, your body and mind never got the chance to loosen their past level of anxiety. The best way to tell whether stress is getting to you is by monitoring your behavior and listening to what your body has to say. Here are the most common stress signals:

- Headaches
- Tightness in the neck
- Loss of appetite
- Excessive eating
- Indigestion
- Forgetfulness
- Depression
- Loss of confidence
- Loss of interest in sex
- Trouble sleeping
- Feeling keyed up
- Feeling preoccupied
- Anger
- Hostility
- Quarreling

These are most common, but, we each individual receive unique signals in our bodies. To begin developing your personal stress mug shot, start by thinking back to the last time you knew without a doubt that you were stresses. May be it was the day your boss harangued you in front of the department employees. Did you have a headache the rest of the day? May be you went home and screamed at the kids. If you write the signals down, will they remind you any of the stress signals without apparent cause, you will know something is bugging you. Then you can begin examining your environment for possible culprits.

The Four (4) biggest boss's Stresses

A. Feeling of helplessness:
For example, you knew what was causing the problem in your organization, but you are helpless and due to the structure and authority, you do not have, you let the problem continue.

B. Urgency
Employers do manage a life of urgency. They go for long lunches, play golf for long hours, and tend to relax for a long period. They do a lot of activities in several moments. The worst part, is that there isn't one of those tasks not marked urgent.

C. Uncertainty
Management expects a rule of performing decisions based on the uncertainty. Which could be a challenge to the employer who does not operate with certainty decisions?

D. Overwork
Since bosses do not punch in clocks, they will not identify overwork and busy. That line is virtually not there. They work for achievements and as such they could be in a constant stress without knowing.

How to Beat Stress: Stress management technique 1.While there is unavoidable stress, there is also stress we create ourselves.

Solution: observe those people in the same likeness of you, and compare yourself with them, the way they handle stress. Exercise should be a routine ie. not extremely strenuous but fairly good to pass over time and minds ie. simple walk distance, yoga and playing games such as tennis.

    Prayers and meditation
    Swimming and cycling
    Visit with active and recreational professionals

In summary: positive and negative stress is a constant influence of all of our lives. The trick is to maximize the positive stress and to minimize the negative stress.

Photo credit by author.

Justine Pool was one of my visitors who came to see me from Uganda. She was a cast and her father was from Italy but was married to a Ugandan Woman. She had a law degree, but her days were few since she had no visa. Somehow, I did not have visa either, and so she had to move in with an American Citizen who had a citizenship, and so she went with him. It was a disappointing history as anybody alive at Idd Amin's time had to run away for his life. For that scenario, a good number of us did not have visa although we were living in America. Without a visa, you could not be allowed to go outside US and if you did, you would not be allowed to come back in the country and neither was you allowed to work in the Country. If you were lucky, you would be given a visa to work but not for a long time, and subject to be revised from time to time and you were not allowed to cross the border coming back in the country. That's how a good many of us failed to bury our parents ie. Mother (1986) and father (1988).

REVIEW QUESTIONS

1. What kind of life style was the King of Buganda?
2. Why is religious another form of political party in Africa?
3. What role did Serina play in Luyirika family destiny?
4. Serubira Mulanie, how did he protect the laud of?
5. What memory children did Kato "twin" had before his death in 1971?

CHAPTER VI

DR. KHIWA-KIWUWA BESTOWED TO GLORY AND THE PRESIDENCY OF OVER 1-2 THOUSANDS MEMBERS OF INTERNATIONAL SCHOLARS AND PHIBETADELTA

(FIRST AFRICAN TO RULE SUCH A GROUP IN DIASPORA)

Professor Edward Kiwuwa Khiwa was born to an African family of Baganda. The family of Erisha Luyirika It could be said that, he was the pioneer in all Africans and black American family to be the helm of the Presidency of such a prestigious organization in the World. There was always a saying that, African race would not contribute to global civilization. Fallacy and false assumptions about the black race and the African continent of which Professor Edward Khiwa, Kiwuwa over took.

Professor Khiwa, in his arguments, he states that, Africa's history did not begin in slavery and despite the peculiarity, horror, and duration of the enslavement of Africans; slavery occupies a minor time frame. In the 120,000 years, of African history, it is in the last 50 years much has been done to combat the entirely false and negative views about the history of Africa and Africans. In actual case, slavery was not carried out in all areas of Africa i.e. Buganda where Uganda's name was emanated.

The slavery of African is much worse than the Holocaust of Hitler's' legacy in the global history of the World. The climate of civilization that existed before then is now forthcoming and is observed as a unique climate to the dominance of the white racist persona. Professor Edward Khiwa appointment to the helm of this leadership of PBD is a testament of this fact. . Yes, slavery reduced humans with culture and history invisible from historical contribution; mere commodities to be traded. From the Holocaust or Maafa the hierarchy was born which continues to govern every living human where race continues obstruct) privilege and opportunity.

Line of Heritage of Grand Parents:
Katangaza (Nutuba)
(Kikonge, Kiwuwa, Butaganya)
Dfossiga of Mpungu, Ndiga Totem
Headquarter at Namaicofu, Mityana
Governed: Professor Edward Kiwuwa, Khiwa
Profession: Professor and Medical Law
Sub. Clan Memebership: 60,000 Members
Katangaza, Kiwuwa, Kikdnge- transferred from Bule.
Date of Restoration to Rightful Administrator: July 24, 2011
Executive Action was taken by:
Ibrahim Sekawu, Segwany (Head Clan)
Ibrahim Musoke, Mpungu (Prime Minister)
Luyirika (Acting Prime Minister)
Kyaaka (Secretary)
Katete, Kayemba (Sub-Clan Totem)
Sewava, Sermbiri
(Honorable: Mengo and Representative his Higness the Kabaka of Buganda)
Lineage of Heritage in Mutuba- Katangaza, Kikongo
Dr. Kigeya, Joshua and Luminsa, Vunyi for origin of Katangaza
Balengera Entebbe; Kigongo
Bugabo; Bernado Kiwuwa, Malunga
Natajja: Masaka; IDD Walungama
Wanda: Jim Kibuka (Kamwokya) Kampalayd
Bony Serunkuma (Sewagnde)
Peter Serunkuma

KATANGAZA – SUB – NDIGA CLAN
Grand Parents Heritage and Lineage of Namakofu, Mityana

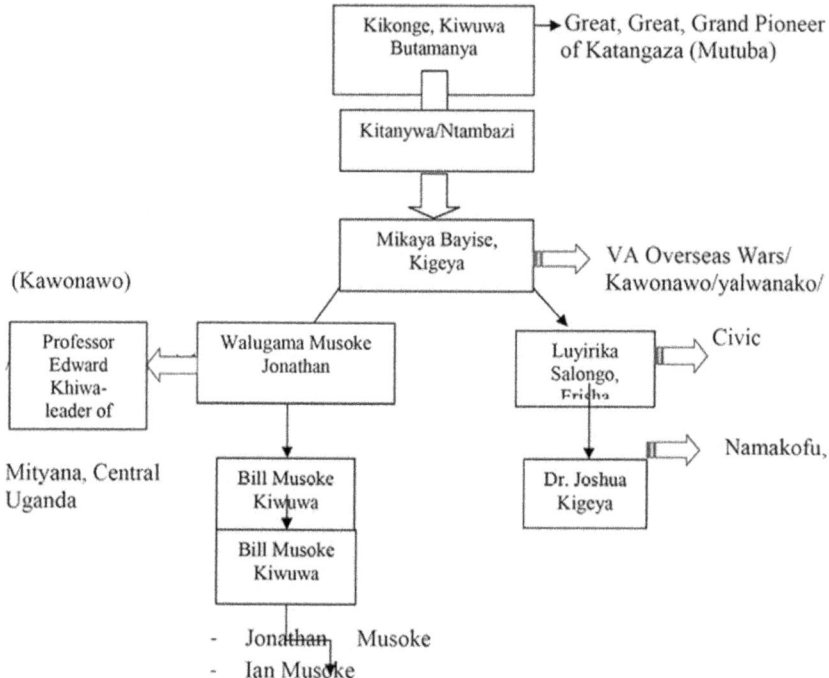

Katangaza kikonge, Mutuba, was left in the document of the "will" of both my parents: Jonathan Walugama Musoke, and his brother Erisha Luyinka Salongo, in which they charged and challenged all grands to claim back the Omutuba –Sub-totem of Ndiga clan from Bule, that was confiscated by our grandfather Banadawa who agreed to keep/give it back to the rightful owners if they were to show up after the religious civil wars that was taking place at that time. Incidentally, "Kyaaka" the grandson of the Pioneer of the Mutuba died of heart attack and as such, one of our great grandfather Ali Mpungu Banadawa, came from his usual home at Kyenajjanja and came to claim the piece of land taken away from the deceased Kyaka who had just died. The elders however, at that time, could not welcome to take over until he proved that he was going to give it back to the rightful owners if they were to show up after the religious civil wars. He had to bring the bones of one of the brothers of Kikonge, Butamanya, and Kiwuwa and had to bury them at the local area, but, with understanding that, he had to participate to restore the institution of Muluka sub-Ndiga clan to the rightfull owners if they were to comeback. Apparently, at his dealth, on his last few words to his successor our uncle Saad Kafumbe and told him to affirm he would back the Omutuba to the rightful owners that had now been residing at Namakofu, Mityana, SSingo. Therefore, uncle Saad who was the successor of Grandfather Ali Mpungu Banadawa, similarly when he had been invited to officiate the occasion of installing the successor of Jonathan Musoke, Walungama at Namakofu, refused to take over the occasion since the rightful ruler of Katangaza was Luyirika the next in line to Jonathan Musoke, Walungama that had just died. But, Luyirika Salongo responded that, he was now getting old, but, if the children who were now studying abroad in overseas Universities outside Uganda, if they were to come back, they would take over their rightful Mutuba sub-totem of Ndiga clan.

Ibrahim Mpungu Musoke the prime minister of the head of the SSiga (highest stage next to head of Ndiga clan), and the Head of the SSiga by the names: Mpungu Sekawu Segwanyi, reviewed the records and research focused to the grands of Kikonge, Butamanya, and Kiwuwa in the line of Kitanywa to restore this leadership. It was a great occasion for the people to witness that, the prime minister under his immediate hierarchy agreed to announce the restoration of the leadership to the grands in the house of Namakofu, Mityana, SSingo. It was a great jubilation, and happiness to all circles since it was done at the ocasssion that held place at Bugabo in the home of one of the uncles of Ali Mpungu, Banadawa. Yes, it was the home of our grand, grand, Yakobo, (James) Balengera. The occasion brought people from all over the World to witness the announcement and people to know each other.

Professor Edward Kiwuwa, the son and grandson of Kikonge, Butaganya, Kiwuwa, was announced the rightful leader of the Mutuba and had to be restored by planting the bark clothe tree at Namakofu, Mityana in the home of the kawonawo Mikaya Bayise who had been a worrier and had fought overseas and so he had been buried at Namakofu, Mityana. Professor Kiwuwa, a worldwide rod scholar had been a leader in Buganda in many occasions. He was one of the children of both Jonathan Musoke Walungama and Erisa Luyirika Salongo, with his mother Nalongo.

Professor Edward Kiwuwa, is an international scholars carefully appointed since he was a group leader and his administration, recognized immediately the proper line of the children of Kikonge Butaganya Kiwuwa. He availed their leadership to lead the children of each line born from the Kikonge Buteganya, Kiwuwa. It should be remembered that the occasion to restore the Omutuba, was witnessed by the members of Buganda Kingdom from Mengo and Hon. Serubiri represented the Katikiro, and the Kabaka of Buganda. It was a colorful occasion that witnessed trampets, drums, flutes, dances of various cultures. It was also the occasion for recognizing the return of the joy to this group of people that had lost their glory for the last 130 years.

The lines of the grands of Kikonge Kiwuwa are: Wanda was led by our uncle Jim Kibuuka at Kamwokya, and Bonny Serunkuma from Entebe near Airport, Uganda, and peter Serunkuma of Kamokya. All the three are holding the flag of leanage leadership of the Wanda one of the children of Kikonge Butamanya, Kiwuwa. Basically, have humble beginnings from Kabulasoke, in Gomba. The wars of Islamics in Butambala made the parents move to that area, and so this line of the grands of Kikonge Butamanya, Kiwuwa was finally established and the toll of our grandparents is set up at the Cemetary of our humble beginnings i.e elders such as : "Kyaaka"," Yokana Njuba for Jim Kibuuka", and Bonny Serunkuma for "Sewagude". The auntie Nakatude and her elder brother at Entebe play a big role to strengthen this Mutuba.»Malunya Bernard for Serubiri Kiwuwa at Bugabo and Kinobe for Katete are holding the mental of the line of grandparent Balengera who was buried in the same cemetery at Bugabo on Entebe road. They are the source of our joy since in this home it is whare the announcement was made by the prime minister of the ssiga Halj Ibrahim Musoke and the head of the sub clan Halj Ibrahim Sekawu Segwanyi whose father was also

Sekawu. The secretary of the occasion Mr. Joseph Kyaaka, played a unique role in keeping together the grands of this SSiga or sub-clan of the ssiga. Mr.Bosa Luyirika who is acting prime minister since the bonfide Halj Ibrahim Musoke is sick and invalidated, though he is still active with minimum effort. But, July 24th, 2011 witnessed the takeover of the Mutuba at Namakofu under the witness of the acting Prime Minister Mr. Bosa Luyirika.»IDDi Walungama from Nantajja the son of Kikonge Butamanya Kiwuwa, he is the head of Nantajja and all the offsprings of our uncle "Mpungu" at Masaka. All the great heritage of the memories to this great father and grand Kiwuwa, Butaganya, is headed by our IDD Walungama. He is also the prime minister of the head of the Omutuba of Katangaza. He is in charge of the cemetery our grand at Bugonzi, Masaka road, 77 miles.

Luminsa, Vunyi is the deputy prime minister of the Katangaza. He is the leader of the Lunyiriri (Leneage) of Kitanywa who was buried at Katende. Yet, Dr. Joshua Kigeya. A reknowned international scholar and the successor to Erisha Luyirika Salongo he is the one in charge of the Cemetary of our grandfather Mikaya Bayise of Namakofu, Mityana. Mikaya Bayise fought overseas wars during the invitation of the colonial leaders in Uganda. He had outstanding records in triumphs against his enemies. Dr. Joshua Kigeya is in charge of the Luyirika legacy and reminants.»Bill Kiwuwa was the success of Jonathan Musoke Walungama. They are all buried in the Cemetary at Namakofu, Mityana. His successor is Jonathan Musoke who resides in Los Angeles, California, and his youg brother Ian Musoke lives in Minnesota….. He has my grands named by my names, "Kiwuwa."

They are products at Namakofu, Mityana, where the headqurter of the Mutuba of Katangaza is officially located….. Under the administration and leadership of Professor Edward Kiwuwa, and it is a herriditary leadership position.May the Lord keeps our leader Professor Edward Kiwuwa … Long live!

REVIEW QUESTIONS

1. Who of Luyirika family was aprfrused captured?
2. What is subtoten of the luyirika children?
3. What are the qualifications for a leader being in Buganda kingdom?
4. Describe the characteristics of the valley of tears in Luyirika's family?

CHAPTER VII

THE DAY OF THE NIGHT DANCE

"The cannibalism and witchcraft behavior" It was three in the morning when three of us my daddy, my young brother and myself walking through a banana plantation under a bright moon. We were heading to the town market which was located fifteen miles from our home. Apparently, kept my father who had a market merchandize waded on the bicycle, I and my brother, were each carrying a basket of tomatoes, and banana leaves on our heads.

At first, it rained on our way, but because we had this load on our heads, it sheltered us from the pours of rainfall. However, father who was always walking a head of us with his bicycle of loaded cargo had to use a banana leaf to protect him against the rainfall.

The equatorial rainfall pours cats and dogs. It indeed poured a lot that night. Several times, we hide under the banana plantations, but not a while a lot did it help. In any case, we survived and moved on until it was over and continued to the town by the name Wobulenzi.

Off course fifteen miles to someone with automobile is not much even at night time. But on this occasion it was not only a long showery rain downfall, but it was also a nightmare since on this day. I met face to face with a night dancer, and a witchcraft man who had carried on his back a dead body of a man who had been buried in the banana plantation we had gone through. At eleven and my young brothers was nine, we both feared dead bodies, not to mention to pass by a grave yard and cemetery of dead bodies. We dissociated with stories of people that had been identified to roast fresh of dead bodies and hold bones of their victims at the back of the roofs of their homes. What My father told me at three in the morning

NIGHT DANCER, A NIGHT TO REMEMBER.

The man with a dead body on his shoulder. The man is running with a dead body extracted from the cemetery or graveyard at three in the morning during the height of the night when everyone is deeply asleep. I was ten under the mercy of my father's protection and me and my younger brother, we were scared of the dead bodies and monsters, and my younger brother was eight. The night dancer holding a dead body and is heading to a safe location where he could have all the bones of the dead body. The night dancer turning a dead body for dinner using the power of the winds crafted with spiritual Satanic authority. We were hiding in a banana plant under a bright moon, the moment was tense and quiet that the night dancer did not see us.

As mentioned earlier, my father was our protection, so walking in the early night and in the morning to look for better place for the sale of our farm market, it meant to sacrifice our sleep and dreams of the night. As Winston church hill prime mister of England once said, —Truth must be protected by a bodyguard of lies, ‖ to this story it could sound within the above statement, and yet, it is a virtual truth. It indeed happened as we had just completed the pouring rainfall, and not long had left a few yards from the burial ground of the man we both had known; certainly we went through the banana plantation scared.

Introduction of a human Dead body for first time to our life as teenagers

We had been scared for all along, me and my young brother to fear the dead body. When elders talked about it in the family settings and other gatherings, I always fumbled. It so happened that on occasions when death happened to the village, I was all the time nervous and could not pass a night without a dream of the deceased, especially if I had known that person before the death. In the early days of life I never viewed and was scared to look at a dead body. I had a sense of anticipation that, he and or she would wake up and take me along with in such along deep sleep equal to that of a monster. So, at the death on the village and neighborhood, I could not walk alone, and neither obeys any one to send me out for long assignment away from home.

On this day when we almost met a night dancer, the story had been told by elder siblings that, night dancers work at night and they held super power of devil that guides them to remove the dead human beings out of the grave. In actual sense, this day, since the burial had taken place in the afternoon in banana plantations which had the foot paths to our farm markets, we were very shocking to wake up and too, pass close to the cemetery and grave yard of the dead.

Of course, we were with our father and the moon was bright in the sky. Certainly, you could see anything including a human being in a distance. Our father, carrying the market sales, ie. Bananas, corns, and I carried a basket on my head full of tomatoes, and my young siblings had a banana leaves on his head. Yes, on that day, I was scared and nervous. However, at three, that is the time when everyone in the village is fully asleep and yet, that is when the night dancers go to the grave yard to pick up dead from the grave. It was in addition the time we had to cover that long journey to secure a good place at the Farmers' Market. Before we left home, father had to make sure we had a spire and a big knife or locally known as a panga.

He asked me since I was the oldest, not to tell anybody that we had those protection devices, and also cautioned both of us, that, we were walking so late at night, it was necessary to wear dark clothes so that an animal and enemy would not easily identify us. Never, sing near grave yard, neither do coughing since that could be an opportunity for bad devils to follow us all the way on our journey. The rain had just stopped almost an hour ago when we finally arrived within vicinity of the grave yard. However, the footpath to the Market was a few yards away from the Cemetery.

We were told by father, that, this is the time to set a sigh of breath since we were now in the district and very close to the burial ground where our neighbor on the village had been buried. As mentioned earlier, we had to move slowly and with no noise that would have to wake up a dead body that was buried in that banana plants. As I came close, just a few yards to the grave yard, my memories could go back and forth to the dead body. I could see the dead in his folder of the bark clothe, in which they betrothed and engulfed his body before was buried, Of course, the bark clothe is equal to a white sheet in which other times a dead body is buried with. Though the custom of burying the dead is slowly fading away in the funeral activities of the urban communities, in Buganda, it is the sign of a happy fair well and a respect to the death. In Buganda Kingdom, one of the regions of Uganda, burial had to be in the bark clothe and the richer and wealth one was, so was the load of the bark clothe. I could remember that entire story in my minds as we were coming close to the burying ground of the dead of the previous day. At around three in the morning, we came close to the scene, but we did not reach it.

As the moon was bright, the banana plantations were also scaring for anybody to walk in them. — be quiet and stop still, do not shake anything', our father who was walking in front of us with his bicycle carrying sales, whispered to me. I wondered what he had seen. It did not take long; the dead body was being whisked to the back of the night dancer. At first, the power of swift wind closed in and chased our observation as the night dancer utilized his magic power to uplift the dead from the ground and carried him to his back. My father advised me that, this is a unique experience since too he had never come across such a moment. He continued to whisper, that, when a night dancer picks up his victim from the grave, does not want any living human to see what he was doing. That, in case if he had seen us, he would have asked one of us to lift the dead body as picked up from the ground and help him to lift the dead to where he would ask you to carry the dead body. So the moment was tense. We down in silence as too were all dead. I lost my conscious, and father used his power of authority as a leader to galvanize us to stand again on our feet and moved forward but in a different direction. I will never forget that hour and that moment, for it scared me and made me a man that was ready to face the World. I asked my daddy what the night dancer was going to use the dead. To which, he answered that, in this world, there are people who eat other human beings as dinners. They on the occasions get visited with super powers of authority beyond their ability. Such people tend to participate in human worship and keep the bones of the dead for passing on fortunes in return earns a survival. Such, people are in different parts of the World and are used as earthly gods that give wealthy, children, and escape of the bad fortunes.

He mentioned to me that, since his family was a full Christian background, he was happy. That his life style never believed in such magic power, though, Satan can give a supper human power, but, a Christian belief disavows all such elements. We continued on our journey, but we left the market early to pick up our previous memories and sleep.

REVIEW QUESTIONS

1. How does anger and guilt affect your ability to reason and how best to handle it?
2. Why do most people work to control their anger?
3. How can you facilitate the release of grief?
4. How important is "crying" a major function for rehabilitation of loved ones?
5. How can anger and guilt affect your personal sub conscious mind?
6. What is stress "reduction"?
7. Who is a victim of stress?
8. What are the most stressful signals?

CHAPTER VIII

THE PHILOSOPHY OF TRADITIONAL AND NON-TRADITIONAL HEALERS:

BELIEFS OF VARIOUS SOCIETIES' AND EXPERIENCE

According to overview on Medicinal Plants and Traditional Medicine in Africa; in all countries of the world there exists traditional knowledge related to the health of humans and animals. World Health Organization the definition of traditional medicine may be summarized as the sum total of all the knowledge and practical, whether explicable or not, used in the diagnosis, prevention and elimination of physical, mental or social imbalance and relying exclusively on practical experience and observation handed down from generation to generation, whether verbally or in writing. Traditional medicine might also be considered as a solid amalgamation of dynamic medical known-how and ancestral experience. The interest in traditional knowledge is more and more widely recognized in development policies, the media and scientific literature. In Africa, traditional healers and remedies made from plants play an important role in the health of millions of people.

REVIEW QUESTIONS

1. How do you compare the Aztec Kingdoms to that of the present Buganda Kingdom?
2. How did the Kingdom of Southern American lose their power and identity?
3. How could you protect the glory of the Kingdom of Buganda?

CHAPTER IX

MY EXPERIENCE AS A STUDENT IN FORMER SOVIET UNION

(Moscow University, Russia & Xarikov State University, Xarikov, Ukraine (Former Soviet Union In Early Times))

The soldeir keep people to escepted to another town you have to have vista to go to another town After four day of traveling by train men and women where tire. They would no lets us get off the train to relack thinking that the citizen would excepted and stay in those town or never hood we all reached at border the train stopped there where building ready to welcome all of us. So that one side of that build was divided for men and other for women. Because we all equal we were told to take off all our clothes and every put it on the box. The receiving security to keep each one clothes in the box, each box where given a number. The women and men had to walk side by side on the walkway and on the ramp toward the building to take hot shower. Coming from Africa and many foreign students from other apart of the world had mixed both White Russia men and White Russia women naked. Everyone took off the clothes and stay to move there naked. At first, the foreigners were nervous to take of their cloths but we are comforted that Russia was the friendliest people around the world. The Ukraine and Russia women were intended to be one friendship off human being so were the Russian and Ukraine men. Since I was born from African among this group of Soviet traveler had never seen anatomy off different of human being naked. At one time I stop walking ahead and gagged at man who was at front of me walking naked and that when I appreciated God act creation of man. Other people who were walking with me in the group. One of them asked me —man of God‖ you are focusing on one man in front of you but we are in here look the same nothing missing because we all the same so he push me toward to move on. All of us walked half kilometer to the build that had hot water we had people waiting for us and again women has hot water. Then after that we each came back naked again walking on the ramp together as you can seen on the picture and then come the to the train and they didn't want us to disappeared in the neverhood, we stay after we when with train to the University student hostels we study Russian language all nobody could speak English except sign languages. After a few months we learned the language ofcause they have match us with beautiful girl who could speak only Russian language and we had to imitate their action and the pronunciation of the word. The great underground of Russian metro-train

We left the state of Ukraine by train came back to study our regular cases at Moscow University. We had to use public transportation most of the time to move around the city of Moscow of cause Moscow University is located in one the greatest cities of the of the world and most to the people in that city used the Russian Metro-train underground of Moscow is one of the greatest wonder of the world ever made by human being which I admired by all human being. The train was contracted in the ground about ten mill in the ground its one of the greatest wounded every human being should have to look at. It is when you are outside on the street of Moscow you cannot reg they are village of building shop and restrant, hospital which may have been build five mill in the ground which connected to highway that link to great on the top outside the city life goes on as the city doesn't had other city below it. The city was design to saver every winter and ballistic missile and explosive tonic to bomb. The Metro-train in the ground move at the fastest supertonic nose and it is always on time to meet the schuldual to the next station no delay of any kind.

ROUND TABLE TALK WITH DADDY & MOM

On the eve before I left Uganda, I had a round table discussion with my parents and their life experiences. The discussion was the last, and the most memorable I remember about them as I never saw them again. My father asked me, — what was the most dramatic experiences that I had met in life around the World? 'I replied that, they were several: I outlined them this way: Survived the cannibals. I told him that, there were places I visited in Africa, where cannibalism was a way of life. They eat you alive if you do not understand their skills in communicating with outside World. One day, it was raining, I stayed away from rain and hid into a neighborhood home. He let me sit down. Yet, the surface had a mat covering a big pit of about ten (10) feet. When I and my friend were greeted each with a chair to sit on, I did not sit down, but my friend did. Apparently, I had just moved out to clean the banana leaf that had been watered with rain. When I moved back in the house, I could not see my friend with whom we had come to escape the rain. I came back just in time to find them fixing the mat again and could not see him. They told me that he had gone. I said: gone where? I was, and had been in the front door of the front house. There is no where he could have passed. So, I ran as fast as my legs could carry me shouting to the top of my mouth. "John, John, where are you? For that was his name! When I reached to a resting, relatively a crowded neighborhood, I was asked about the other boy I normally move by, and why I was sweating on such a cold day! That's why I told them where we had hid the rain. To my sorrows, I anticipated that, I had left him there since I did not see him in front of the path and yet had run very fast. They all in unison, agreed that, that, home was a human meat eater. That, possibly, that's where he could have been some one's dinner and on the statistics of human cannibalism records. I did not know what to think of it. I was young about twelve to thirteen years. From that time, I refused to pass through that country path any more coming back home from school. What a history I remember. It seems it happened last night! It really meets the days of our lives. For the life is a journey we make and escape every day....But, how we do it, is a survival for every human species on the planet. For each one has a day of birth and a day of death! John left the world and nobody could have a trace of him! What a world we live in!

Walking naked with no clothes during the Soviet Union time. During the early 70's, Soviet/Russian government made effort to unite friendship around the World. I happened to go to study on the Friendship scholarship at that time in the Soviet Union at the boarder of Ukraine and the Republic of Russia after arrived by train for four days. ..... My Daddy and Mom laughed when I told them that, in Ukraine at the time we arrived in their State from Russian State boarder by train, we were told to get out. We walked about half a mile naked. We had travelled for four days by one of the swiftest train on the face of the earth! When we reached the sauna house, they forced everyone to carry their clothes to the store keeper to keep them for us. I was totally scared. For I had never been in such a tense! I had never been naked in the public. But, for Russians, that was not news. They forced me to take off my clothes and had to stand in a line and go to the place to freshen up with warm water. As you notice in the photo above, all those people on the rail are naked and are going to take shower. The Women had their side and so were the men. The Russians believed that all men were equal. There were no reasons why men should not walk naked. Man, I had a chance for the first time to observe the anatomy of the human being: Big, small, rough, slander, etc. Yes, that's when I recognized that, we are human beings and was created equal! Though it was a challenge for a small boy from Africa to move in the crowed of whites and others from around the World as students, it definitely was a lesson to learn.

The Great underground of Russian Metro-train: I told my Daddy that, if there is any mystery man has hidden in this World, is the Great Underground or Metro train of Russian train system. Built in about twenty miles deep in the ground and surrounded the entire City of Moscow of about 30 million people. On the surface you cannot see this system. The shops and other high rise buildings are above the train system. On the surface, you could see only electrical trains, buses, trucks, and all human activities. You cannot imagine that in below twenty miles is the Greatest Metro-train that covers the

City about hundred miles radius. These trains are as fat as a lightning. In a second the train may cover sixty miles for the pick up at the waiting passengers at the underground metro-station. Everything is controlled by the electronic system. The radar and control panels are monitored from one remote control. The doors open automatically and no one is allowed to stand close the door when the train is charging to arrive or it's taking off! It's extremely swift and very long of about quarter a mile. What an opportunity to monitor and look at one of the Greatest Wonders of the World.... The Great Metro train of Russia or Soviet Union as it was that time.

The Lenin's grave and his body imbedded and left at the surfaces and the exchange of the guard of Leninis' body. Lenin was a great leader of Soviet Union that led the revolution of the people of Russia into the system of Communism. Lenin believed that, all properties belong to the community of the living population. It was not fair for one to have more than the other. If one has more than the other, it is because he/she got it through exploiting. They believed that human effort should come from each individual contribution to society. They did not believe in free enterprise as it is in the United States. Lenin believed that when bread is grown, it should be shared equally. Lenin did not believe that slavery was essential for humanity to be rich. That's' why there has never been slave trade in Russia as it was in the Countries of Southern Europe and Mediterrerian sea. The people of Russia worshiped him for his brilliant ideas. His ideology of communist system, transformed the people of Russia. Since I came from a free enterprise economic nation, I did not care too much about it. But, the ideology was taught in schools, universities, and all walks of human life in Russian and other Republics they had won to make them the fifty two republics of Soviet Union. Lenin, when he died, was embalmed and kept in glassy outside for people around the World to come and watch the power of human brain. Yes, Lenin was and left a history and a Mark for people of Russia and other communist nations. When you observe the picture above, you will see the body of Lenin in the glass in the room where it had become one of greatest source of revenue to Soviet Union. Lenin expanded the Soviet Union to bring the nation into fifty two Republics.

Of course, when he was gone, other communist party chairmen became active in politics where the end results were to weaken the soviet empire and each Republics became a nation of independence. Premier Gorbachev, was the last leader to cement a farewell blow to the history of Leninism and Marxist system. The great giant which was a quartet of the World, is now striving to become a pure economic capitalist system. We went in the line and stayed in line for two days till you could reach to see the body of this man! Here I asked, what makes other people great and live a mark in history, while others leave no mark to remember them. The body of Lenin is an example of the Uniqueness of our human civilization and history of man. Lenin teaches us that, it is not what you do, but what legacy do you live for future generation to remember you! Great people have gone in history, some with a human mark such as the leader of the Great Republics of Germany. "No one on humanity will ever forget", he caused the loss of twenty million people and it is marked in all streets of Russia and the largest un marked graveyard cemetery in the World, located in the City of Leningrad, the last gate boarder City to join Helsinki the capital of Finland. It was such an experience to be a part of such history.

How did you get together between mother and you and your arrival at Namakofu, Mityana, Uganda? Here I wanted to know how my father met my Mother! I told them that, they had heard a lot from me, now it was my time to ask them a few intimate questions to which they gave answers as follow. Some answers were academic to me and others were regular human discussion with their child. My daddy had to have a wife after he found out that, the Mother of his wife belonged to the same clan and also had refused to change to Christianity. They had two children the girl and boy before they split and had to marry my Mother of sixteen years of age. They stayed together and had a jubilee of fifty years in Marriage with a number of children and a significant of them died while adults and had been principals of Secondary schools and others as administrators in government institutions. My Mother studied home midwifery from the Missionaries that she had befriended with other members of the same Christian faith. Many times, she delivered herself with many of my siblings before she could go to the hospitals. Father was well educated and was a translator for the Missionaries. Would you elaborate on each of the subheadings mentioned above? My father exclaimed. I said to them, I will but briefly.

Survived the cannibals

Dig up the graves to pick up the Dead bodies using supernatural power

In some parts of Uganda, there are a cliché' of a few whose behavior and acts reflects cannibalism. They either dig the grave of the dead and pull out the dead body and utilize some parts of the body as pieces for dinner and left over such as bones and skull is saved for the rituals of the family to use it to give blessings to the community and followers.

Being trapped in some ones home when it rains

Usually in some parts of the same neighborhood as mentioned above may trap their victims for dinners by using sophisticated methods. If say, you are escaping the rain, the grounds and parents always warned us not to go into strangers home to escape rain. The tricks were that, the owner would dig a deep trench in the center of his home. It would be as deep as six feet down. On the surface, ie in the sitting room, he/she would cover it with a rug, and smoothly looks natural as smooth as the rest of the sitting room.

At the rug, he/she would position a chair so that you would assume that it is a safe ground to sit on. Apparently, when you step in this house for the rain, he would welcome you with a comfortable sit in the house. As you get yourself comfortable and sit on the chair and or stepping on the rug, your body would be succumbed into the trench and the deep pit that was prepared for its victim.

As the rug falls inside deep into the pit, the owner would rapidly take control of you and become succumbed into the list of dinner for that home. Parents and grandparents, tend always to warn their children, especially those going and coming from school not to get into home of strangers, and they do not know. Once, it happened when we are out of the school and one of my friends, who had gone with me to escape the rain, was soon disappeared as he sat on the chair of that home.

When, I saw that, I ran away from that house and ran running in the rain till I reached home. It was a scaring situation, that, up to now, I remember as if it was yesterday..... It is a warning, not to visit or eat food from strangers' and neither just visits homes.

> Night dancer currying his dead body victim for dinner Walking naked in Soviet Union at the boarder of Russia and Ukraine. It was a long journey from Russian Republic to Ukraine. It took four days

> Travel by train. All men, boys, girls and women on this journey, were tired as we reached the boarder of Ukraine from the Moscow the Capital of

The great underground of Russian metro-train

We left the state of Ukraine by train came back to study our regular cases at Moscow University. We had to use public transportation most of the time to move around the city of Moscow of cause Moscow University is located in one the greatest cities of the of the world and most to the people in that city used the Russian Metro-train underground of Moscow is one of the greatest wonder of the world ever made by human being which I admired by all human being. The train was contracted in the ground about ten mill in the ground its one of the greatest wounded every human being should have to look at. It is when you are outside on the street of Moscow you cannot reg they are village of building shop and restraint, hospital which may have been build five mill in the ground which connected to highway that link to great on the top outside the city life goes on as the city doesn't had other city below it. The city was design to saver every winter and ballistic missile and explosive tonic to bomb. The

Metro-train in the ground move at the fastest supertonic nose and it is always on time to meet the schedule to the next station no delay of any kind.

Vladimir Linen the Favorite Son of Russia (Soviet Union)

Lenin was the greatest leaders of Soviet history (Russia). His personality and charisma, made the movement of Russian population to lead to conquest of many nations that became territory of Soviet Union under one philosophy of socialism communism. His movement attracted millions willing and unwilling to be subjugated to the whiz of exclusive casual of commissar society. He believed everyone was born equal and so nobody should own more than the other. If one had more than other it should be shared to those who have little or nothing. Lenin's existed at the time when there was famine in the country due to world war and internal war in the country. If the family was to produce bread or food it had to be brought and shared together. If one had more clothing should be shared equally. That meant that no one owned anything. Everything belong to the state. So he is regarded in history as the grandfather of Soviet Russia. Of cause during his time he left the Soviet empire which was equal to one half of entire world. When he died, nations around the world, sent delegations to view the body of Linen. He was the Chairman of the Council of People's Commissars of the Soviet Union. His body in the glass view used to be protected by the guard of honor. The guard of honor used to change shifts from time to time. He died January 21st 1924, at age 53. Vladimir Lenin and Stalin: A lesson for human leadership and ego (April 10-Jan.21, 1924). The moment Lenin stepped into power, he knew what he wanted. All along, he stated a proletariat Revolution which had been based on political and economic principles of Karl Marx Fredrick Engels. His plans were soon supported and led by the Germany Bolshevik Revolution against Russia's constituent assembly, which by its decree, dissolved its constituency. Leninism economic principles and political agendas were immediately implemented. Stalin, the colleague of Lenin, admired his economic agenda, inspiration speeches and characteristic persona, Stalin, in extension of what Lenin had began, when got appointed in power as well, he declared himself — the god of the sunl, meant that, the party represented by everyone in the country, would deliver equally to all citizens like the sun is to all under its power of light.

He ordered the Moscow Metro-railway system be designed, that, all its stations should be designed and decorated for all citizens to look up and admire the fruits of the Great Russian Political Party. Yes, Leninism was the political economic system of all Russian great new Society and empire. The Great Metro-train of the City Moscow, was an achievement and a testimony of one of the Lenin's economic plan for the nation, but, implemented by Stalin as the Secretary of the party. It was the party's manifest to introduce economic electrical system distributed across all territories of Soviet republics under the Communist Party.

The Failure of Stalin against Leninism economic system: The nation went under deprivation and economic down side since starvation was felt everywhere in the country. There were lines of people looking for the rationalized food in the Market. The Party blamed Stalin and his leadership for causing failure against Lenis' economic system that he had implemented, but only that, Stalin miss guided its applications. The nation outcry the death of Lenin, but, not the death of Stalin. Lenin's body was laid to rest, but, until recently was never buried, and millions of people from around the World had to come to Moscow and view the body of their great leader. His body was installed in glassy for protection and had to be guarded by the soldiers at different shifts. The shifts were organized under guards of honor system. Linen's body, the Moscow Metro train, are one of the eight (8) Great Wonders of Russia and the World. Visiting Russia, leaves one to wonder the human power of architectural design.

SUMMARY OF THE CAUSE OF DESTRUCTION OF CIVILIZATION OF A SOCIETY

At the beginning of this text, discussion was made to the sources of what made a destruction of strong kingdoms and empires to disappear with their civilization. Great civilization of empires, kingdoms, societies, and human creative machinery of civilization have come and gone. The great civilization of Societies such as Egypt, Greece, Empires of South America, The Soviet Union and its mighty power, and other kingdoms big and small around the World, have extinct. So are the great leaders of strong nations and weak, equally have disappointed their beneficiaries. The author wish to position himself, that causes of the decline of civilization of society and as mentioned above, is not coming only from conquest of wars of one country against another such as conquest of England and neighborly kingdoms to ultimately United Kingdom and form of English culture, by submerging other European cultures, but also is due to disunity that originate out of the inequity of rights and opportunities which is mainly responsible for the degeneration and decay of civilization relative to other parts of the World. Inequity in sharing resources, crept into the breakdown of cultural values of the survival of the Kingdom and great established societies such as the former Soviet Union. The cultural influences from other societies (ie. Internet) ; imported cultural influences to the king dorms, empires and Great societies, do destroy the cultural status quo of those communities and their established structured systems of their empires. As the Great Soviet Union society tasted the outside world culture in productive materials, and other international cultural influences of the twentieth Century, the society began to integrate causing the newly republics to continue forming their own nations. The faulty though could be avoided for temporary, it became increasingly difficult to stop foreign goods and services come into the country and inter-marriages of the foreigners, ended mixing international languages with soviet (Russian) and forced within locals to disintegrate the status quo of former soviet and leaving the Republic of Russia in a nation of its own. If all other kingdoms and empires continue to be infiltrated such as that in Soviet society, and other kingdoms of the world, would end up serving the pluralistic society divided under predominantly privileged and unprivileged classes. This usually cause the rich and poor grading society. If not properly managed do result in the decay of civilization , chaos, riots and change in attitude against the populous ruling class. The surviving kingdoms, and societies have to adjust to the cause of outside influences that ends up destroying the cultural status quo! That's how the Soviet republics, empires of S. America, Egyptian civilization, Greece, and many other more including the British monarchy, and Buganda kingdom in Uganda lost their major authoritative glories of admired civilization. However, by monitoring the effects discussed, such societies could restore their glories with authority and dignity. The families have lost their traditions and cultures by not observing principles discussed in this paragraph, and my father emphasized this point when he was directing me to emphasize his memories and philosophy to the world.

THE TEN GEOGRAPHICAL WONDERS OF THE WORLD: BASED ON (UNESCO) RECORDS

In my adventure of the World, I have had the opportunity to appreciate the beauty of nature and what, the humanity, characterized the — Ten (10) Great Wonders of the World: ‖ The Egyptian Pyramid system, Cairo, Egypt, Africa

The City of Moscow, Metro- Railway system, Great Republic of Russia, Eur

The Grand Canyon of Arizona, Arizona, USA
The Great trading Center of the City, of Chicago, in USA
Niagra Falls, USA, the great Falls of USA
Mt. Everlast ... the tallest mountain in the World
River Nile, the longest river in the World, Uganda, Africa
The Great Wall of China, China, Asia
The Mississippi River, USA
The Gayers Springs of hot Water, USA

The Great Kasubi tombs of the Burial of the Kings of Buganda, Kampala, Uganda. These grass-man made huts, have lived for many Centuries beyond

The Great train of Siberia

Apparently, I have had the opportunity to tour and viewed these natural wonders of the World. They are indeed wonders of the human and natural beauty and genius. 13.The Palawan island beaches and Sanjuanico Hwy of Philippine across the Pacific Ocean. You drive across the water of Pacific as you eat your lunch of "Adobo the main dish of Philippine. It is a combination of chicken and meat and or Pork and chicken. These were the great minds of the great scientist of Philippine Island. The foundation is so strong that you can drive side by side in the central of Pacific Ocean. It connects three major Islands. Starts from Samar Island, to Leyte Island. Manila is located in Luzon big Island of Philippine. But, sanjuanico Hwy begins from Sama Islands.

THE TEN (10) GREAT UNDERGROUND METRO-TRAINS OF THE WORLD:

Moscow: opened in 1935 with 11 KL (6.8miles) it was the first underground railway system in the Great Soviet Union. Currently, its route length is 301.2 km (187.2 miles) the system is mostly underground. It has ridership of 6.55 million daily.

Tokyo Metro –train system: Jointly owned by private and Japan's government.

Seoul South Korea train system ⸺ It has a ridership of 5.6 million, and mostly used train in the World.

Mexico City –train system- The second largest Metro system in North America, after New York City Sub-way, and in 2008, the system served 1,467 mill passengers and it has a daily ridership of 5 million passengers.

New York City- metropolitan transportation Authority (MTA) It is one of the oldest and most extensive public transportation system in the World with 468 stations in operations. In 2009, the subway delivered 1.579 billion riders, averaging over five million on week days.

Paris Metro system- Is one of the densest metro networks, with daily riders of 4.5 million.

London- Its underground, metro train system serves large part of Greater London and neighboring areas of Essex, Hertfordshire and Buckinghamshire in England.

London Underground (1863), was the first underground railway system in the World. In 1890, it became the first to operate electric train. Despite the name, about 55% of the network is above ground with ridership of 2.93 million passengers. Osaka, Municipal sub-way- Metro net work in the City of Osaka (of Kansai Region). It has 125 out of the 1,108 rail system (2007) in the Osaka-Kobe-Kyoto region, and operated by Osaka Municipal Transportation Bureau. It opened in 1933 with ridership of 2.26 million passengers.

Hong Kong's railway net work — The approval has been secured for the merger of MTRC and the Kowloon –canton Railway corporation, following discussion to merge it for economics of scales and effectiveness.

St. Petersburg Metro–This is an underground system in Petersburg and Leningrand oblast Russia. It has been opened since November 1955. Due to its geological, the Saint Petersburg Metro is one of the deepest subway systems in the World, and the deepest by the average of all the Stations. The system serves nearly 2.2 million passengers daily, and it is also the 10th, busiest Sub way in the World.

REVIEW QUESTIONS

1. How did colonialism affect traditional foreign empires?
2. What was the cause of lode spread epidemic disease?
3. What is hedrqes and give example?
4. Who was Ibrahim Mbungi Masoke in Luyirika's family?

CHAPTER X

INTERVIEW WITH MY PARENTS AND SIBILINGS

ROUND TABLE DISCUSSION 5:

How did you come together as my parents and here in this Village at Namakofu, Mityana, Uganda?

As we were close to visiting each other on this round table, between my parents: mother and father, I asked several questions which held interesting intent.

Mother and Father's response on Questions: —Why Most Marriages fail and Divorce? I asked this question since my mother was concerned that, it was taking too long to have grand children from this world adventure's son. Father replied:

Marriage & love Relationship- A complete Marriage.

He outlined what made their marriage lived to over fifty years, which to him it was a good record, even though others stay together longer than that.

He outlined four categories of love that are robust for a successful marriage: First, outlined them and then discussed each one to the level that, each one binds in to form a complete marriage:

Agape love
Phileo
Storge and
Eros. ... Then he began to discuss each one as to the following:

A complete marriage; a gape love A marriage relationship is built over a life time. There are four kinds of love needed to make a marriage relationship complete. They are as mentioned and outline above. All of them are essential in marriage. Agape is the highest form of these types of love. Agape is love an unconditional. It loves when all other types of love quick, and care when there is no apparent reason to care. This love comes from superhuman control and or from god into a person when they are centralized with a Christian and a temper of self control.

Phileo love – is the kind of love that makes an agape love enjoyable. Phileo love is having tender affection toward your mate. Most friendships are built on phileo love… Phileo is that ― something‖ that you see in another person that draws you to be their friend. It's the enjoy of friendship, successful marriage has to have for the husband and wife to be tenderly love (Phileo)each other while they overlook each other's faults and failure (agape).

Storage love- Is another type of love required in marriage. Storage is a physical show of affection that results from a pure motive. It may be a hug, a kiss, or another expression of genuine affection. Because males are different than females, the wife usually needs this kind of love more from her husband. It is important for the husband to set aside his need of a companionship and meet his wife's main needs, which is affection.

Eros love- is needed to make a marriage. Eros is the fulfillment of physical sexual desire that a husband and a wife show toward each other. It when ―the two‖… become one fresh.‖ If a husband fails to deliver this level, a wife may usually be attempted to get it from somewhere else, thus a precursor for divorce. However, when all types of love operate in a marriage, the marriage is complete. A picture of a complete marriage is a husband and wife who laid down their life for each other (agape love) no matter how many times the other offends them or the other, and or causes them to have ill feelings. They, both have tender affection toward each other (agape love). They enjoy each others' company because they are best friends. Because they enjoy each other so much, they hug, kiss, hold hands and do nice things for their mates. (Storage love). Because their hearts are filled with agape, phileo and storage, a warm passionate desire arises within both of them to enjoy each other sexually (Eros). None, that kind of God-Centered marriage will weather any storm.

We must nurture and protect all of these different kinds of love leaves agaping hole in our relationship. Lets' remove one type of love at a time and see how incomplete the other three are alone. Agape love is unselfish, for the thing that will be prevalent.

FAILURE OF MARRIAGE AND LOVE RELATIONSHIP

Daddy when during our round table was addressing the question of divorce in our society, he said: In modern time, 90% of marriage and love relationship is due to family and individual up rising, and uplift social ethic mobility. Poor family upbringing is mostly noticeable in the tenacity of marriage and home survival. Apparently, marriage failure is a consequence to fail to resolve conflicts, infidelity, and lack of ability to adopt to relate to: family economics, love of children, and failure to govern in-laws and respect and trust with ultimate understanding that, a man is — a bread winner‖, head of the family, and a wife is his other side of life who champions the success of her husband. Both couples have duties to do in a specialized form for the home to be happy, respected, and prosperous and succeed in social communities.

ANGER MANAGEMENT & CONTROL PERSONALITY

Our time has social challenges due to ownership of properties and material motives. No marriage commitment is noticeable at lengths. Daddy however emphasized that, our society rewards those who have more materials than those who have little. Therefore, the greatest challenges of humanity are how to control anger. A good number of inmates in jails and prisons are due to lack of anger management and so goes the family and divorce in marriage. He said that, in his time, marriage meant a commitment for life in spite of challenges in home. When he was asked how to manage anger he replied that at many times he and his wife would be angry to each other. But, we always had to patient to each other. — —Patience is a virtue.‖ He exclaimed! He continued to explain, that anger is a process of learning to recognize signs that you are becoming angry and taking action to calm down, and deal with the situation in a positive way.

How long have you been married to each other? I asked my parents. Daddy affirmed that their relationship in marriage had just begun with sixty years in marriage, he ended!

Then, I turned to Mammy, "I am about to go, do you have a last word to your son?" I humbly asked. She replied to me that, as she was sitting quiet on the table, she intently took note of what my father had spoke and affirmed that, I took those last words seriously that they could possibly be the last words. That, their bodies (my parents body), were both tired and grown! She felt that she did have many days for her left to live. She cautioned me, however, that, if I were to hear news of her passing away, I would not be surprised that, there were talking to me fairly clear that, since I was going away to America, it was not a nearby place where I would drive by in an hour to provide medical treatment! That," I should bid farewell to them now, you will never see us again." She exclaimed! She reversed however, that in case you will never have a chance to be at the funeral and burial service of the occasion, you will remember while in America, the love of me and your father, we have given you when you were with us in our domain. She mentioned that, all her loved ones to the family should read the 2 Timothy 4:6-8 and that was also the last text father agreed with Mother to pass to the World and go with it to the United States.

Are there Angels? She asked me if I had understood what she asked. She told me that, if I were to believe that, there are angels, then, when she passes away, her life and that of her husband will be restored in heaven, and that the angel will come and visit me while in America a few days after her funeral. The conversation was so tense, that, I would protest the rest. But, she emphasized that, she was preparing me for eventualities! Sure, me and my Mother were so close .... For a Mother and a son! In a moment notice, she went in the house and brought a sweater and embraced me and emphasized, that, this was her sign of love to me and bade me farewell! Yes, in the morning, I woke up early and took an early tax car to the City in preparation for departure to America.

On arrival in America, it took four Months, and I was informed that my Mother had got a stroke. She stayed in the hospital on and off and ultimately, and after several Months, she had a massive stroke and passed away. The news of her death affected me immensely! I was laid in the hospital for two WEEKS. When I was in my house lying on my bed, there was my mother and she asked me how I was. I could not believe it. I cried. Mom, "Are you alive?" She said, "I promised to visit you in America". Here Aim, I have come to see how you were doing after you left the hospital. I could not believe it! I woke up, and stood to embrace my Mother as I saw her when she was still alive. She made me farewell and told me to have a good sleep, the, I would come back if necessary! I went to bed again, and never show her again, except to dream here and there but not as this event. I asked my father on the phone, are there Angels? My father who was alive at that time, said, yes there were angels, and you must believe in them and feel them. But, then, I remembered the words of my senior brother who was together at that round table. He emphasized that, God was everywhere in every religion and it was we human beings that glorifies in mate materials. That, whoever believes in Jesus Christ and his second coming, would see his second resurrection. Joseph Agway, who I was next sibling, passed away, as a Christian member of the catholic Christian community. My Mother and father raised us as Christians but of different denomination. My brothers' words at the round table have come to live. Anyone who dies a Christian, will be raised again if the deeds before death were of Christ like!

I remember, I asked one more question to father: "How would you feel since you were the surviving siblings in your family and the only lasting of them all! My father, replied that, "yes, my siblings a majority were members of the Moslem faith, but, I decided not to be a part of that! The faith you chose to grow and die under, will always protect you and fellow believers will always be your brothers and sisters. However, he reiterated, if I were to do it again, I would have shown all of you my children the foundation of your heritages. Now, that you are in different parts of the World, I do not have opportunity to show you members of my family that belong to the non Christian, but, Moslems. He emphasized that, 'my leadership would be necessary to galvanize all family members of all different beliefs and bring them to the family of blood brotherhood. That, if I were to do that, my family would be threefold strong! Today, we have done what our father asked us to do and were are strong since blood is stronger than faith of religion. However, in memory, my Mother had ended that since the family had sixteen children, the last should strive to close the curtain with the faith of the parents that began that family, and we should all strive to meet during the day of resurrection of His second coming..

REVIEW QUESTIONS

1. What is the role of bark wire in Uganda?
2. Describe the day of the night dance with history of the Luyirica"
3. How courageous were Luyirika's children during their day of the night dancer?

BIBLIOGRAPHY

Thomas Nicholas, Colonialism's Culture: Anthropology, Travel, and Government, Princeton University Press, 2011

Organization

The book is organized into eleven (X1) parts of chapters. Part 1 represents is a result of a 36-month process involving five family members and three international family friends. It has been a privilege and honor to work with each and every one of them: my brother Dr. Joshua Kigeya, in US; a colleague in the State of Arizona, Tracey Prater my godly father in Tucson. Tracey Prater took me in his wings when I had no sponsor and stranded in the hotly desert of Arizona. He was of the age of my father, and liked to brag of him replacing my father in American continent. Stephen Prater his successor always reminded me that in this world, we all belong to the family and God's race. Here an African black young man received such a hospitality grace from a white American family that had never known me and background of my parents. The family took me in his home, ate and shared his children's food and slept in sitting sofas of his sitting room, it was an extraordinary love. This was also a reminder of a great family, a man and his wife. They lived in Stockholm, Sweden. We had just left the church service together, invited me to their home and had luncheon. The weather condition changed, they had one bed in one bedroom, there were no way they could drive me back to the City. So, they gave a hot shower, and after, they shared their bed with me. On one side were his wife, and the husband slept in the middle with one big length winter blanket of the Swedish winter weather. They made sure that, nothing could happen to me and they did not want to be sick. Oh, what a memory and exemplary love. Here, they were white, but received me as if I was theirs. The friendship grew until I departed from that glorious nation. Mr. and Mrs. Hahn, you were special to me and will never forget you! Yes, there has been several people I would call my own and special for me. There are people who have left me to be my own: Dr. Clyde Montgomery, vice President for Academic Affairs, and several others who I will never forget..... for through them, I have come to grow and survive in the community of this competitive World.

    I personally dedicate this book to my family, especially, Mr. Iddi Walungama, the prime minister of the kings' line of Katangaza traditional family of Baganda to which I am the hereditary leader in the Ndiga clan totem of the Buganda kingdom, representing his subjects all over the World. Further dedication is extended to my wife Harriet and my children: Justine Nakimbugwe, Godwin Kiwuwa, Edward Kiwuwa, Edwin Mpungu and my other children in Uganda including: Grace, Kigongo, Ronald, Ruth Nakatete, Robin Kagere, and off course, the beloved Norah Kiwuwa, Mugoya. People such as Nasimbwa, and David katumwa and successor to my mother at Kigalama including my great uncle Kalumba (they looked after me when I was growing up, just a kid .... Thank you elder kalumba) Additionally, I wish to thank my friends and colleagues both from the church, academia and world social pleasure. Yes, my beloved parents that raised me up: Erisa Luyirika salongo and my mother Nalongo, Luyirika. They are sleeping in the solitary lands of the tears of the valley of Uganda. My senior brother Erisa Semakula and his family you are always special to me!! Yes, elder Bossa, the clan elder of Ndiga totem to which I belong and grew up, and his assistant Ibrahim Sekawu and my brother Luminsa, Bayise, Kyaaka, Edward Kaddu, James Kaddu and all my great sisters and rest brothers but the whole mountain of thanks goes to my eldest brother and his wife Dr. Joshua Kigeya and his wife Abbey ....Dr. Kigeya is the hereditary leader of our family and the successor to Erisa Luyirika our beloved father who went to be with His glory in 1988. While mistakes from this document may not be easy to escape, though tremendous effort is provided to eradicate them, ultimately, Iam available to eradicate them and any other criticisms would be received with grace! Thank you all!

I thank you all for your unrelenting encouragement and support from beginning to end. Edward Khiwa, Kiwuwa, Professor

CHAPTER XI

THE BIRTH AND RAISING OF A FIRST CHILD IN THE NEWLY MARRIED FAMILY

Sons: Godwin Kiwuwa & *Edwin Mpungu, Kiwuwa

I would remiss if this document was to be completed without the information of my wife and a child in the family with named Godwin Kiwuwa, born to Mother and father Mary Harriet Khiwa. Mary Harriet Kiwuwa, the Mother of our first child Godwin Kiwuwa, she is from the Golden State of Uganda, and from the Buganda Kingdom.

Brilliant as she was, her infectious smile at first sight, was imposed upon her by her Mother Cate Jakira. The family that raised her is from the same home of the neighborhood of the father of Godwin Kiwuwa. Her training in medical delivery apparatus of Uganda impressed all her Christian believers who bestowed upon her "child of Jesus" who heals on the Sabbath and any other vital days of a claim of a patient. Harriet met her husband on his trip from US to Uganda.

It was a love of first sight. A friend of the family made the connection. She stayed at his home since he had married her Sister. Kiyingi, my family brother, was a flamboyant man. When he said something, it had to be done then. So, was on this occasion! He informed the recent graduate in Nursing school, to get ready by dropping all lads that had interest and had to move to a new World.... The move was exciting to this young lady who in addition to learn of United States, had already got a glimpse of the brilliant young man from her neighborhood.... With a title of Dr. Edward Kiwuwa. Finally, Edwin Mpungu, with a great smile was born to this family and the joy of the Kiwuwa's multiplied. Both, young men have grown to be gentlemen of the community and society in this global challenges.

The next day, when the Professor was on his way back to US, with so many choices introduced to him to select someone to be his life companion, so did he MS. Isabirye, the great dear friend made the introduction and connection. This was a beginning of history for the restaurant in which the first conversation took place, gave us all three, a free drink.

A reason was, they knew I used to sit in that restaurant and met my friends, but, of them all, none were ladies. This was a surprise to them all, and so the owner who joked with me all the time, with questions of whereabouts of my wife, decided to promote this conversation that had been started between the three of us, by honoring, and blessing it with a free drink of Pepsi and Coca-cola. She was a quet then, and the sip of the drink was no more than two minutes and she gave up. She let us complete the rest for her. The conversation of the first love made the clock slid slowly and before we knew three hours had passed by us. We covered all topics from earth to heaven including the structure of the family the creator would bless us with. Jokingly and with a humbly smile from a soberly of coca cola, I advanced the conversation of who would be the names of our first child. As if she had thought of it and knew it in advance, she inniated the first name of her eldest brother: "Godwin." She asked me not to consider any other name since I was going to select his last names as it is done in the Buganda Kingdom culture.

The children automatically take on the names of their father. We took two years after her arrival in the new World, to recognize that, I was going to be a dady and that, when she brought up the names, though I had forgotten, she could not forget.....so on his birth day, the agreement was resurrected and so we confirmed what the great creator had recognized our natural gift of our love for each other.So dear readers, everyone has a story, but what is your story for the love of your first love!!

GODWIN, KIWUWA

This was the first child of the couple together. It was a baby of their youthful lives. It was an exciting moment when the doctor announced in the hospital, that, he would be a boy. The Mother, this was her first child. It was to be a preparation and ecstatic anxious waiting for nine (9) Months. The events folding would indicate a major important relationship of love. Here a new human being was now to be born to this recently married couple. Both were not aware the type of a child was to come to the World. I could see that level of commitment since each couple had never gone this far. The selection of a good physician, (obstrics and Gynecologist), was extremely crucial. This would have to go through all phases of nine (9) Months. It is this doctor who would determine the quality of life for both mother and the yet to come baby.

Loving to the Moment of birth was a challenge

As months were folding, I could observe a constant monitoring of both the infant and Mother. I was an assured the type of the baby would look like. During the sixths and seven Months, commitment to each other is very paramount. The Mother would be asking questions: what medicine should I take? Answer was always, "No medicine." The Mother to be was entirely depending to the love of the father. The selection of a good hospital clinic and insurance coverage was an important element to prepare for the future of these couples. It was very important to understand procedures of a highly risk clinic. As the sixths and seventh Months, are potential period of Pre and clampsia. The parents, ie Mother and father have to understand each other well. Beds, bottles and toys were to be bought in advance in preparation for the baby.

Selection of a name: What is in a name?

Several weeks passed by and this pacient couple was looking to the moment of labor and discharge from the hospital. Meantime, several names were being tossed up.

The great news of delivery was forthcoming since the mother had been in custody of the baby to be born; the father was getting excited every passing day. "I am going to be a daddy." I exclaimed to the audience that wanted to know more about Mother and our first child. Of course, the clinical and ultrasound had already identified the baby that he woud be a boy.... Meaning I would get a fellow man hood in the house.

We were a happy couple but for the two years, we spent together, there was no sign of forthcoming of a child. Yes, a baby is a gift from the Creator of lives. It's one of the rare opportunities hidden away from humanity of both a man and a Woman. From this experience, I learnt that no one should ever take each partner especially Mother for granted. Mothers go through a lot. The nights are long for them, and temper, tend to change and hospitality of them change as well. Some Mothers to be may usually break away from you and would communicate better with some one else other than you the expectant father.

Mothers to be may not like to be ignored neither consider them on the list of other Women, you are familia. This period before the baby is born, is an hectic moment. During the latest moments of labor, some women may ask to eat at a constant basis and yet others may eat food you never anticipated then to eat.

The first time father, have to have a support from friends, cousulars and relatives around for encouragement. On occasions, however, the mother to be usually is more beautiful than at other times in history. Giant clothes and maternity preparation is a great moment of seeking for each other and love.

To be a torerrant father to be is the name of the game. The Mothers to be at some time, may not like to stay with fathers to be, to be around her. It is that type of moment where at some times the Mother to be, needs her husband, and on the other hand, she feels she could do without! Those moments are tough to the father to be especially young parents. Because, at one hand they feel that, if ignored she or he can always have another sweet-heart… or whatever!

Again, a child is a gift that should never taken lightly. . How many women and men seek for the child and somebody to be a child in the home, to have joy to their lives and could not be successful. Sometimes, the father may have weak and less sperms, yet on the otherside, the woman could be barren.

The parents minds are always never stable: "will the child be born with deformities, will the mother damage the ovary during pain and labor, and will be born prematury? How about still births? All these minds run to and fro in the minds of yet to be parents. The greater side, is the defective genes, hereditary diseases such as sickle Cell; and or down syndrome.

Other major challenges: The father being the head of the family, has a responsibility to determine the methods of up keep and raising of the baby. When the mother to be is due in the clinic, the father has to strike off all protocols before in preparation for the arrival of the baby. At this time, when a lot of fathers find this newly baby, unable to deliver for him and the mothers, they quetly go to another town, district, to escape the wrath of responsibility. Leaving Mother and her infant. Now, that is very bad! The names are crucial as you move close to the labor and delivery of the baby.

RELATIONSHIP IN LOVE DURING LABOR AND DELIVERY OF A BABY

Two kinds: Internal and external love and feelings of one another. Most people have external feelings and love of each other. But some would prefer and care but does not love the force of internal love.

Internal love and feelings for one another. The internal love is a hidden and secret to relationships of one another either between a man and woman or whatever form of love. This is intuitive and internal commitment to each other such as my wife. We may argue and debate each other, but the core fundamentality of our constant commitment has to be a robust catalyst for our relationship to keep on moving one proverbial foot after another. It does not depend on outside, but internal love. **"WHAT'S IN A NAME?"**

Parents usually assign their children names based on several reasons: Parents, especially in most developed countries such as those of Western World, tend to assign names of their children based on names of their heroes, if a boy and girls, the most famous women that have contributed greatly towards survival of human kind.

This position, could be current or women of history. Parents that are in this category tend to assume that, their children may as great as those national heroes and famous. There are familiar names that parents do tend to assign their children (names such as : Kennedy was a great leader and charismatic; Joseph, he was a survivor of his brothers and saved his family during crises of the femine, Jacobs survived challenges with is brother (Esau) and was the father of children of Israel, and yet some others give names to their children based on the achievements of their activities and leadership during wars eg. Macarthar; Abraham Lincoln; David Livingston, with Geographical Society of England and others such as Stephen, a marter in the Bible etc.

Human beings, "we are a product of our ancestor." For what they eat, love and names they use to call of ech other in memory of the legacy they left to each other after they left this world. So, parents, be careful and take time to consider the names you give your children. They will make them great or they will demote them in their domain society. Here Godwin does not know where his names came from, but they are either opening the door for him and wild opportunities…. But, this overall depends to the choice of our parents of what we do not have control over! Chose the names carefully to avoid your child from being abused and not properly recognized in the society.

Respect: A well though out names, do have a potential to give recognition and child potential to community woes and global challenges.

But, regardless of fame, no parents give names to famous people who are failures and weak in the society. For istance, names such as Hitler a general of great Germany during World War II, is a name never given to somebody's child; and so are names of heinious crimes of disliked people in history, such as, Idd Amin the former General and president of Uganda.

Names are assigned due : Parents' Culture and Backgroundin Buganda Kingdom... ((Bugand Kingdom is the largest tribe in Uganda, have a kingdom and King, whose kingdom is in the most Central Part of Uganda and the first Region in Uganda to receive a University by the English Colonial Powers.)

In Buganda Kingdom, Parents usually give names to their children based on their culture and former country of origin for either mother and father. Mexican may assign names based to their culture and heroes and former relatives in Mexico, and so are the Russian, the Swidish, Africans and many more others. So, whats' in a name? It is everything that identifies that individual from the society and fellow humanity of the World.

Culture of the Buganda Kingdom (the Baganda) in Uganda. Parents assign names to their children due to the culture and background of their parents. In Uganda, culture do determine as who assigns the names. In Uganda, if the grand parents were alive when the child was born, it is the duty of grand parents to assign names to their grand children.... It is the grand parents that have such authority. In the kingdom of Buganda in Uganda, (Africa) names chosen for the child must have a meaning, and are selected from the parents totem – clan.

The children in Uganda are assigned names based on the side of names of father, but not of the Mother. The names must come and belong to the totem line clan of the father. The names of the clan the father comes from, determine the names of the child. Godwin Kiwuwa, my first son, of our marriage with Mary Harriet, belong to the fathers' clan ... locally known as the sheep (Ndiga). Everyone in Uganda, especially in Buganda Kingdom, must belong to a clan to qualify for the title of one of the subjects of the King of Buganda Kingdom. The kingdom of Baganda as called majority of the subjects of the kingdom of Buganda, must each belong to a totem.

The head of the totem is the King of Buganda. There are fifity two (52) totems in the clan of the people of Buganda kingdom called the Baganda. The Baganda are the majority in Uganda of the population of over thirty million people, but the kingdom has over eighteen (18) million of the Baganda speaking Luganda as the names of their language called. As mentioned, ealier, every individual person in Buganda kingdom, is called a Muganda, and must come from one of the fifty two (52) totems, headed on top by the King of Baganda (majority of the subjects of Buganda Kingdom)

The lines of the Baganda totems are governed by the hereditary rulers of each totem of the Kingdom. The names of each totem were line up, thousands of years ago. The names and kind makes a great difference in Uganda. In Uganda, you are identified by totem, and clan which is usually a Muganda or Baganda Plural)

If you belong to the parents that come from one of the totems of the clan of Buganda kindom, then you are a Muganda. Since each totem has a distinguished list of names, no names from the list of another names of a totem, can be assigned to a child who does not belong to that totem. Because of the specialization of names in a totem, the child's name must be selected from this particular totem of his father. The individuals with names identified from each totem, in the Buganda Kingdom culture, such a person you share the same names of the totem, he or she is your brother and oryour sister. Such people cannot marry each other and by virtue of the same totem list shared names, are mebers of your family. By same token, they are not only with the same blood, but you must recognize each other as mebers of the same parents regarless if they have met or never met before.

If children of the same names coming from the same clan and totem, marry each other, such marriage does not have legitimacy, and is subject for prosecution by the prevailing government and judicial authorritty..

The children of Dr. Edward Kiwuwa: (Khiwa). They were born and assigned names based on the above principles. Kiwuwa Godwin and Mpungu, Edwin their youngest son, belong to the list of the (Sheep .. Ndiga) clan of the Katangaza totem of which Dr.Kiwuwa heads that totem. The significance of the system and totem in the Kingdom of Buganda, the system has protected the value and interest of the Kingdom. People of the same totem and clan cannot marry each other and do so to avoid in bleed of cross blood. The system has reduced several hereditary diseases known to man today; during the existence of the period of Buganda Kingdom' s existence of the over five hundred years.

Campaign to Prevent Teen and unplanned Pregnancy, childbirth, trained attendants.. the Midwifery etc

The research made by my graduate Medical students at institute of public Health, Kampala, reaveled some of the causes of un planned pregnancies, child bearing and delay of childbirths.

The study revealed several reasons in response to the above. It revealed about five reasons in response:

> It wa noticed that, Africans same in other places observed, had average age childbearing was, younger than the average for marriage.It emphasized that, by age 25, 44% of Women have had a baby, while only 38% have married.

> It was also observed that, most births happen out of wedlock. It was identified that, 48% of all first births were from unmarried women. It implies a new move for the society as to determine a new demography. Most un wed Mothers were not teen Mothers. Delaying childbirths, is attributed not only to the teenage (23%) of unmarried births were to teenagers as to sixty were to women in their twenties.

The study also revealed that, 39% of cohabitating couples who had children break up within 5 years. And nearly 40% of cohabitating had a baby in late 2000 and 2005 had spliup. By the time their child was five; that's three times highr than the rate for twenty something parents who were married when they had a child.

Finally, the Kiwuwa's family is young compared to the national average age in relative to the parents average age of childbirth. Raising of a child takes caring, and a level of torerance and adulthood stamina. Children are raised with love and assured to have a great academic future. It was due to the parents worldwide education. Neverthless, there are challenges to family planning especially in African and those from the developing nations as opposed to the industrial nations.

CHALLENGES TO FAMILY PLANNING IN AFRICAN SETTINGS (UGANDA)

A. The deficit of Primary Care Providers

On average, a Uganda Midwifery delivers between 350-500 babies each year, which is double the recommende number (175) by WHO. The required number of trained Midwives in public Health facilities in Uganda is (15,606)but only (4,607) of possibilities; causing a high infant Mortality. Over 800 women die everyday world wide from preventable causes related to pregnancy and child birth, accrding to WHO and youg adolescents face a higher risk of complication and death as a result of pregnancy and childbirth compared to older woma. Every day, twnty women die in Uganda, a country of my former humbly beginning. Maternal and infant Motarlity during and childbirths is significantly high.

Family planning programs have not been a great success story in these socities of the African World due to: The high rate of maternal and infant Mortality in African and emerging societies.

The second reason for not being successful program is due to: the African Continent is vastly undeveloped with plenty of opportunities to have a stable household income and daily food of varities. Parents usually have a vast piece of lands, they pass on to their remnant children; though we need to practice industrial intensive farming of the 21st century.

The level of family prestige: It is a great error if a family does not have large families. The number of children in the home is the prestige of the African home. The father is awarded a great prestigebefore his peers if is considerd a man of a big family. Raising children in African society is a survival for the fittest.

The members of the society you belong to, have a tendency to look after their own. If a father and or Mother does not have a strong financial resources, chances are such a family and may be a selected few are left behind and will be illiterates. Especially, daughters are ignored and between a son and a girl, a girl . with limited resourses, daughters have always not educated and not placed in institutions of higher learning. The fathers have on occasion reasoned that, a daughter will find a husband and look after her, but a son is to look after his households and in most cases may be the fathers' heir and administrator of the estate and in care for other siblings.

Although daughters have on occasion done the same, but, arguments has been that, they do not stay long to keep father's estate since men will always look after them or if they do not go with them, the men will take away the estate from the family. Yet, today, educated daughters have played a significant role in the development of the estates of their fathers and development of a nation.

Take, Norah Kizza Kiwuwa, my daughter, was well raised by her uncle after her father passed away. Her uncle (Dr. Kiwuwa) pushed over his elder brothers' family and protected the estate. The children went to institutions of higher education with mentoring and financing of their Uncle, Professor Kiwuwa.

Today, Norah Kizza, is at the rank of Mayor of a great City in Uganda, Africa. All this success of the family would not have happened if the uncle had such a poor image of understanding daughters as great leaders both in the family and citizenly. People from all over the World, now come to consult this young lady on how to do their jobs. Kagere Robinah Ntabade: This is a typical daughter who should be example of others. The Uncle (Dr.Edward Kiwuwa) assisted her, but she put in more funds by hardworking doing her spare time and succeded to get school fees. How I wish all children that orphans would imitate this young daughter who you can view her photo inside the text. She went through nursing school and completed master's degree on her own with virtually little support. This is a typical example of orphans that have beaten odds in the 21st century.

The significance of children to the families in African and other societies:

In Buganda Kingdom, a married man and a woman, with children, are respected and are considered in highly esteemed positions in civic lives of the kingdom. The kingdom is fully aware that, a stable home, makes a stable kingdom and the greatness of a nation. The kingdom and the people of Uganda and in Buganda Kingdom in particular, take it serious to every adult man and a woman to be married and have children and educate them too as well.

Cultural Tradition:

However, if a man may have a great home, and with great wives, but if he dies with no children, such a man by tradition, his dead body is not allowed to be passed in the main door of his to go be buried. But, instead, they pass all his remains through back window of his house before the moment of his funeral and burial. Now, again, if on other hand, one had committed a suicide, such a person would not be buried, but would be carried to the thick forest, and tie a knot around him or her and give him or her several beatings and since he had died long time via suicide of him/herself. They would live such a deadbody quetly to the forest all in unison without crying and show sign of sorrow, his loved ones and others and friends would come and camp at his or her home. Sometimes, they would not provide a successor of his body as it is a tradition of Uganda culture to provide a successor to the deceased who is supposed to look after his estate, and to lead the deceased siblings and his widows. Summary: "What is in a name?" ..... A name is your identity and it is all what is known for you to stand for and it is the foundation for a legacy and people yet to come to remember you..... people should protect their names and never give lightly your word to some one, a name is your Identification to the current World, and that yet to come. With a good records of your achievements you do not have an ID for social security because your names is as good as your gold… people have saved others in trouble because of the name recognition. The participation and success in civic national activities depend on your family background, and your name recognition. For that, I assigned my first son, Godwin Kiwuwa, to take on my name recognition here at home and to the world. But, was selected from the totem of the clan led by the King of Buganda to where our lives humbly began. May all readers of this text, enjoy this great background of the Culture of Buganda Kingdom.

Practice Questions of chapter XI

Suppose a cheque of $5,000 was handed to you, to plan your weeding, use a zero base budget to justify each and all activities.

Why is it difficulty to determine the names of human being and what significance is in a name?

It is said in a metorpher: "Like Dady like a son." Discuss what the saying mean to you

Should sons take on names of their Mothers than their fathers or neither, please, explain the significance in a name and the interest for your position on this issue!

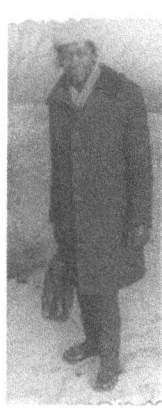

Author at Moscow University, Soviet Union, and other European universities as a Rhodes Scholar. "what a winter season in Europe!" I did not plan for this! I exclaimed as freezing was getting me up to minus zeros. Nine (9) pieces was expected of you to walk in the streets of the, then, soviet Union. Otherwise, the State police had to stop and assign you a ticket as well as picking you up!

It was difficulty to determine if this flamboyant young man would one day be in charge of the international scholars' two and half million scholars.

The parents of the author: (father) and (mother of the author). The parents of the author of this document, (Professor Edward Khiwa) not only did they wish their children to achieve higher academic education, but they involved in the education process of their children. They could do together school homework, work together to schools and sit in classes to moniotor behaviors of their children with others and in relation to their teachers. They were active in parents/teachers and school programs.

Eriya Waswa the senior twin brother at his last primary school. He left a word to workaholic to achieve recognition. He died a prominent leader in Uganda and was well loved by his students. He never liked to play soccer, but as its coach, his scholls and teams were the leading of other schools.

Twins Erisa and Eriya in their early lives as principals and headmasters of primary schools. The two twins seated (rt Eriya Waswa and Left Kato Erisa) were prominent principals of primary schools and well established civic leaders in their respective communities. Their father and Mother, organized their faculty and challenged them aggressively while they were in earlier years of a teenage lives. Kato another twin seated on the left in a suite, had a great command of English languages and an advanced skills in academic cultural diversity Management within schools and government civic agents. He was well liked by his students and administrators. His children were left to complete their education at free tuition and scholarship. The family from which they came from, was humble, as you notice the signature of each ending page of the document.

CHAPTER XII

GRAND PARENTS LAST WORD: THEIR LEGACY TO FUTURE GENERATION

The remnants of the brothers of Erisa Luyirika, Salongo, the father of the author of the "What my father told me at three in the Morning." On the far rt is Sheik Kiwuwa and on RT. Rev. Kyaka. They have contributed to the stability of the history of Luyirika dynasty.

Read the Interview with the elder women:

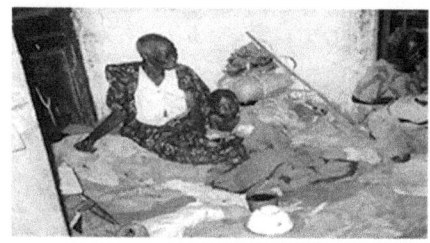

The two great- great parents as you notice them above, have a lot to reveal about the roots and foundation about the family of Erisha Luyirika Salongo. The two lived up to one hundred twenty four and one hundred twenty respectively. They were the surviving siblings of the Luyirika and Jonathan Musoke Walungama, of Namakofu, Mityana, Singo, Uganda. The two lived in the central part of Uganda in Africa. It would have been a remiss to complete this document without exposing their background and a word of legacy they gave their grand children and those yet to come. They were from the family of Mustafa Lugeya, who is resting in the Mountain valley of Butambala county in Buganda King dom. The two women were the remnants of the Kitanwya' and the only surviving of the Children of Kikonge Butamanya.- Kiwuwa whose model is demonstrated in NDIGA (sheep) clan shown on pages 91 of this document. It is of the cleanage of subclan called Katangaza sub clan, today, being governed by Professor Edward Kiwuwa, the Professor In United States of America.

The two women lived together for over forty years. One of them had children and the other did not; the response of how they went through life along with their feelings were affected by the children in this interview.

Does Religion have an impact towards longevity of life? The two women were both Muslim and practiced a Halal diet of no pork and alcohol. They believed that a man should have no more than six women if he can afford to look after them. One of the women mentioned that her husband had nine wives before her. She was the tenth. She trusted no men after this marriage and had no children. This caused desperation when she was old when her sister used to have children and grandchildren. She had nobody to visit her or to talk about the past. The other woman, in addressing this question, said that the religion to which she came into this world from her parents was Islam. That is the only reason she knows. She also said, that it did not bother her when the husband married other women. She had a good choice of a man before marriage. She believed she represented Aisha in this marriage, the wife of Mohammed. Her marriage was by her parent's choice; an arranged marriage. She did not go to school too long after learning the rituals of the Muslim faith incluiding the Quaran and was immediately married off to her husband. Her husband had already had five wives. She was now the sixth. She was married when she turned 16. Her marriage lasted until her first husband died. They had five children together when he died. She then re-married which was arranged by her uncle. Her uncle was 40 years older than her. So they used to go out and he looked after her. He built her own home and raised her children of the other husband that had passed away along with the new one's children. She had three children with her second husband. The marriage didn't go beyond a few years because the husband was stricken by a deadly disease that dates back to the end of the 19th century. It killed many people. The people moved to distant lands to escape the disease. She too escaped and went to her grandparents leaving her husband in another home. Then she had heard that her husband had died.

The Challenges of the 40 days of Mourning.

In an unexpected encounter at a caregiver's conference, I posed a question which I wanted these ladies to respond to: The question was of age, and they felt that during the 40 days of mourning, there was no enteractions involving love with their loved ones. They have to remain celebracy at this period. One of these ladies by the name, Aisha Nasereka, who never had a child of her own: during her day had been icon of beauty, she was actress. She was a goddess of beauty who embodied the charms of youth: as a dancer and singer. She felt, however, that because she exercised herself and fall in love with a brown, tall looking young man during the forty days of mourning, that's why God punished her and denied her an opportunity of a child. This was a period of her mothers death that, she had to have some fun with this young man who had come along way and distance to share bad days with her. So, in return, she had to please him and she felt bad to do so, but that, this was bad in the religion of Allah. Her sister kept reminding her that, marriage is a secrete vow, getting a child, had no relationship with a constant broken marriage with six husbands that she had fallen in love and marriage. However, for her she believed that there was something special in the morning of the forty days. Ofcourse, shesays that, her Mother did notlike it that's why she played to her God that, in return God replied by denying her a child.

God of the winds

As you see beyond the old women at their back, there was debris in bundle saved and kept to please their god. They believed that, there was super-powers that gives success and blessings in whatever one does.She asked me that whoever would be her heir would be passed over the properties of the wind to which I replied that, some of us do not believe in winds. That, such behaviors was the tools of Satan that he uses to control human behavior toward another and that very same person. She did not that I was a Christian, but on this occasion, she told me that since I was young and pride in life, there was much more to study about this Earth. She vividly affirmed that, in all cases, there is power beyond human being which could not be denied. When I asked them to pray before we left them, they agreed but kept one of the debris that gives energy, life and power. When the prayer was over, they wanted to give me something that gives power, but categorically, I refused and decided to disguise myself and with those in my companion that I had come with on this trip! The question I left with these elderly women was: Does Satan have power to do things you do not want to do to you? Is there such a thing as Super-power and the super winds? All those questions carry an insurmountable logic to address. But, to many of those I travelled wit, they accepted: that, Satan exists and has Power and you can evenmeet him in secrete houses where he dwells and provide extra power of authority. Well, I did not believe in it and I kept on loving them as my great, great parents. Did it kept a long time of life! I do not believe it eventhough it happened. When one of the elderly woman that had children, but was traumatized because of the challenges of sorrows she answered this way in her feelings about grief, sorrow and anger.

How anger and guilt affected her:

Another mother expressed her feelings when told that her six year old son had suddenly died because of a congenital heart problem "I went through a series of reactions such as numbness, disbelief, guilt, and anger toward my husband and the doctor for not realizing how serious his condition was".

Anger can be another symptom of grief. It may be anger at doctors and nurses, feeling that they should have done more in caring for the deceased. Or it may be anger at friends and relatives who, seems, say or do the wrong thing. Some get angry at the departed one for neglecting his health. Stella recalls: "I remember being angry at the departed one for neglecting his health. Stella recalls: "I remember being angry with my husband because I knew it could have been different. He had been very sick, but he had ignored the doctor's warnings." And sometimes there is anger at the departed one because of the burdens that his or her death brings upon the survivor. Some feel guilty because of anger-that is, they may condemn themselves be sure they feel angry. Others blame themselves for their loved ones death. "He wouldn't have died" they convince themselves, "if only I had made him see another doctor sooner" or "made him take better care of his health." For others the guilt goes beyond that, especially if their loved one died suddenly. How can I love with my grief? "I felt a lot of pressure on me to hold in my feelings," explains Mike in his father's death. To Mike, suppressing his grief was the manly do. Yet he later realized that he was wrong. So when Mike lost his grandfather, Mike knew what to do. He says: "A couple of years ago, I would have patted him on the shoulder and said, be a man. Now I touched his arm and said, feel however you have to feel. It will help you to deal with it. Of you want me to go, I'll go. If you want me to stay, I'll stay. But don't be afraid to feel. Maryanne also felt pressure to hold in her feelings when her husband died. Borg mike and Maryanne recommended: let yourself grieve! And they are correct. Why? Because grieving is a necessary emotional release.

Releasing your feelings can relieve the pressure you are under. The natural expression of emotions, if coupled with understanding and accurate information, lets you put things in proper perspective. Of course, not everyone express the same way. And such factors as if a loved one was ill and dying. Talking about your feeling to a "true companion" who will listen patiently and sympathetically can bring a measure of relief. Putting experiences and feelings into words often makes it easier to understand them and to deal with them. And if the listener is another bereaved person who has effectively dealt with his or her own loss, you may be able to glean some practical suggestions on how you can cope. When her child died, one mother explained why it helped to talk to another woman who had faced a similar loss: "to know that somebody else had gone through the same thing, had come out whole from it, and that she was still surging and finding some sort of order in her life again was very strengthening to me." What is you are not comfortable talking about your feelings? Following the death of Saul and Jonathon, David composed a highly emotional dirge in which he poured out his grief. This mournful composition eventually became part of the written record of the bible book of Second Samuel. Similarly some find it easier to express themselves in writing. One widow reported that she would write down her feelings and then days later reads over what she had written. She doubts this was a helpful release. Whether by talking or writing, communicating your feelings can help you to release your grief. It can also help to clear up misunderstandings. A bereaved mother explains: "my husband and I heard of other couples that got divorced by losing a child, and we didn't want that to happen to us. So any time we felt angry, wanting to blame each other, we would talk it out. I think we really grew closer together by doing that." Thus, letting your feelings be known can help you to understand that even thigh you may be sharing the same loss, others may grieve different-ly at their own pace and in their own way.

Something else that can facilitate the release of grief is crying. There is a time of weep, says the bible. Surely the death of someone we love brings on such a time. Shedding tears of grief appears to be a necessary part of the healing process. One young woman explains how a close friend helped her to cope when her mother died. She recalls, "My friend was always there". The word process does not imply that grief has any fixed schedule or program. Grief reactions can overlap and take varying lengths of time, depending on the individual. This list is not complete. Other reactions may also be manifested. The following are some of the symptoms of grief that one might experience. Early reactions of grief include initial shock, disbelief, denial, emotional numbness guilt feelings, anger.* Is it normal to feel this way? A bereaved person writes: "As a child in England, I was taught not to express my feeling in public. I can remember my father, an ex-military man, saying to me through clenched teeth. "Don't you cry!" When something has caused me pain. I cannot recall whether my mother ever kissed or hugged any of us kids (there were four of u). I was 56 when I saw my father die. I felt a tremendous loss. Yet, at first, I was unable to weep." In some cultures, people express their feelings openly. Whether they are happy or sad, others know how they feel. On the other hand, in some parts of the world, notably in Northern Europe and Britain, people especially men, have been conditioned to hide their feelings, to suppress their emotions, to keep a stiff upper lip and not wear their hearts on their sleeves. But when you have suffered the loss of a dear one, is it somehow wrong to express your grief? What does the bible say?

Those who wept in the bible

The bible was written by Hebrews of the easten Mediterranean region, who were expressive people. It contains many examples of individuals who openly showed their grief. King David mourned the loss of his murdered son Amnon. In fact, he "wept with a very great weeping." (2 Samuel 13:28-39). He even grieved at the loss of his treacherous son Absalom, who had tried to ursup the kingship. The bible account tells us: "then [David] the king became disturbed and went up to the roof chamber over the gateway and gave way to weeping; and this is what he said as be walked: 'my son Absalom, my son, my son Absalom! I that I might have died, I myself, instead of you, Absalom my son, my son!' (2 Samuel 18:33) David mourned like any normal father. And how many times have parents wished they could have died in place of their children! It seems so unnatural for a child to die before a parent.

How due Jesus react to the death of his friend Lazarus! He wept on nearing his tomb. (John 11:30-38). Later, Mary Magdalene wept as she neared Jese sepulcher. (Jogn 20:11-16) true, a Christian with an understanding of the Bible's resurrection hope does not grieve.

What if you feel like weeping? It is part of human nature to weep. Recall again the occasion of Lazarus' death, when Jesus "groaned in the spirit and… Gave away tears." (John 11:33,35) he this showed that weeping is a normal reaction to the death of a loved one.

This is supported by the case of a mother, Anne who had lost her baby Rachel to SIDS. Her husband commented: "the surprising thing was that neither Anne nor I cried at the funeral. Everyone else was weeping. "To this, Anne responded: "yes, but I have doing plenty of crying for us both. I think it really hit me a few weeks after the tragedy, when I was finally alone one day in the house. I cried all day long. But I believed it helped me. I felt better for it. I had to mourn the loss of my baby. I really do believe that you should let grieving people weep. Although it is a natural reaction for others to say, "Don't cry; that doesn't help".

How some react

How have some reacted when desolated by the loss of a loved one?

For example, consider Juanita. She knows how it feels to lose a baby.

She had had five miscarriages. Now she was pregnant again. So when the car accident forced her to be hospitalized, she was understandably worried. Two weeks later she went into Labor-prematurely. Shortly afterward little Vanessa was born-weighing just over two pounds. "I was so excited", Juanita recalls. I was finally a mother!

But her happiness was short lived. Four days later Vanessa died. Recalls Juanita: "it felt so empty. My motherhood was taken away from me. I felt so incomplete. It was painful to come home to the room we had prepared for Vanessa and to lol at the little undershirts

I had bought for her. For the next couple of months, I relieved the day if her birth. I didn't want to have anything to do with anyone.

An extreme reaction? It may be hard for others to understand, but those who, like Juanita, have gone throug it explain that they grieved for their baby just as they would for someone who had lived for some time. Long before a child is born, they say, it is loved by its parents. There is a special bonding with the mother. When that baby dies, the mother feels that a real person has been lost. And that is what others need to understand.

How anger and guilt can affect you

Another mother expressed her feelings when told that her six-year old son had suddenly died because I'd a congenital heart problem. "I went through a series is reactions-numbness, disbelief, guilt, and anger toward my husband and the doctor for not realizing how serious his condition was" Anger can be another symptom of grief. It may be anger at doctors and nurses; feeling for the deceased. Or it may be anger at friends and relatives who, it seems, say or do the wrong thing. Some get angry at the departed one for neglecting his health. Stella recalls: "I remember being angry with my husband because I knew it could have been different. He had been very sick, but he had ignored the doctors warnings. "And sometimes at the departed one because of the burdens that his or her death brings upon the survivor. Some feel guilty because of anger-that is, they may condemn themselves because they feel angry. Others blame themselves for their loved ones death. "He wouldn't have died," they convince themselves, "if only I had made him see another doctor sooner" or "made him see take Bette care of his health." For others the guilt goes beyond that, especially if their loved one died suddenly.

How can I live with my grief?

"I felt a lot of pressure on me to hold in my feelings," explains mike in his father's death. To mike, suppressing his grief was the manly do. Yet he later realized that he was wrong. So when mike' lost his grandfather, mike knew what to do. He says: "a couple of years ago, I would have patted him on the shoulder and said, 'be a man.' Now I touched his arm and said, 'feel however you have to feel. It will help you to deal with it. I'd you want me to go. If you want me to stay, ill stay. But don't be afraid to feel.'"

Maryanne also felt pressure to hold in her feelings when her husband died. "I was so worried about being a good example to others," she recalls, "that I did not permit myself the normal feelings. But I eventually learned that trying to be a pillar of strength for others wasn't helping me. I began analyzing my situation and saying, 'Cry if you have to cry. Don't try to be too strong. Get if out of your system.'" So Norge mike and Maryanne recommended: Let yourself grieve! And they are correct. Why? Because grieving is a necessary emotional release. Releasing your feelings can relive the pressure you are under. The natural expression of emotions, if coupled with understanding and accurate information, let you put things in a proper perspective. Of course, not everyone express the same way. And such factors as which loved one died suddenly or death by long illness might have a bearing optional reaction of the survivors.

Releasing grief- talking can be a helpful release of death.

Talking about your feelings to "a true companion" who will listen patiently and sympathetically can bring a measure of relief. (Proverbs 17:17) putting experiences and feelings into words often makes it easier to understand them and deal with them. And if the listener is another bereaved person who has effectively death with his or her own loss, you may be able to glean some practical suggestions on how you can cope. When her child died, one mother explained why it helped to talk to another woman who had faced a similar loss: "to know that someone else had gone through the same thing, and that she was still surviving and finding some sort of order in her life again was very strengthening to me."

What if you are not comfortable talking about iPod feelings? Following the death of Saul and Jonathon, David composed a highly emotional dirge in which he poured out his grief. This mournful composition eventually because part of the written record of the Bible book of Second Samuel. Similarly, some fund if easier to express themselves in writing. One window reported that she would write down her feelings and then days later read over what she had written. She found this as a helpful release.

Whether by talking or writing, communicating your feelings can help you to release your grief. It can also help to clear up misunderstandings. A bereaved mother explains: "My husband and I heard of other couples that got divorced after losing a child, and we didn't want that to happen to us. So any time we felt angry, wanting to blame each other, we would talk it out. I think we really grew closer together by doing that." Thus, letting your feelings be known can help you understand that even thigh you may be sharing the same loss, others may grieve differently-at their own pace and in their own way.

Something else that can facilitate the release of grief is crying. There is "a time to weep", says the Bible. (Eclesiatastes 3.1,4) surely the death of someone we love brings on such a time. Shedding tears of grief appears to be necessary part of the healing process.

One young woman explains how a close friend helped her to cope when her mother died. She recalls: "my friend was always there for me".

While grieving, take appropriate initiative: are there errands that need to be run? Is someone needed to watch the children? Do visiting friends and relatives need a place to stay, recently bereaved persons are often so stunned that they do not even know what they need to do, let alone tell others how they may help. So I'd you discern a genuine need, do not wait to be asked; take initiative. One woman whose husband had died recalled: "many said, 'If theres anything I can do let me know' but one friend did not ask. She went right into the bedroom, stripped the bed, and laundered the linens soiled from his death. Another took a bucket, water, and cleaning supplies and scrubbed the rug where my husband had vomited. A few weeks later, one if the congregation elders came over in his work clothes with his tools and said, 'I know there must be something that needs fixing. What is it' how dear that nah us to my heart for repairing the door that was hanging on a hinge and for fixing an electrical fixture!"- compare James 1:27 Be hospitable: "do not forget hospitality," the bible reminds us (Hebrews) 13:2) especially should remember to be hospitable to those who are grieving. Instead of a "come anytime" invitation, set a date and time. If they refuse, do not give up to easily,

SUMMARY AND CONCLUSION

In assement of these elderly women, one deduces that, they really liked the Islamic religion. But, it was not the religion that helped to extend their life expectancy. But, it is their way of protecting their lives. They avoided high risk life style and enjoyed a more solitary lives.

In every religion, beliefs and cultural regions are surviving and long lasting survivors who are not traditionally Islam. Take a district of Seventh Day Adventists in Lomalinda California. This group of believers, practices literarlly the same diet like the Islamic faith. They too, do, not eat pork diet, neither eat meat of any form. The study made a few years ago (25) years precisely found that, their life expectancy was much longer than the national average. The same studies ranked to that from the studies made of the State of Utah from the Mowmen's movements. They also avoid diet with meat and alcoholics. Their life expectancy though, is much lower than the Seventhday Adventists of Califonia, they still rank higher. Ofcourse, public health standards began with nations such as Egpyt, Mesopotanian and all countries around Mediteranian sea. Many of them were of course Islamic beliefs, but their infant mortality is much higher than the Western World.

ASSESSMENT SUMMARY OF A SUCCESSFUL LEADER AND MY EXPERIENCE AS AN ADMINISTRATOR

Photo credit by author.

Photo description: stresses the point on how fathers of Uganda (and the parents of the world as well as politicians and scholars must learn the process of becoming an administrator) address their children and family during a time of crisis. Here I was demonstrating to my children to grow and survive against international challenges and behavior. As leader of the clan, people all over the country listened to my challenge of how to survive HIV/AIDS, chronic diseases, and risky behavior — to survive and be productive in the 21st Century. The qualities of a successful administrator is to depend upon 3 important ingredients: 1) conceptual principles whereby people notice will notice your decision making process; your decision making history reflects your current work 2) academic and scholarly principles is where people critique your academic achievements and the ability to use it to solve needs of mankind 3) human public relations where people recognize people who deal others in everyday life of employment, at home with the family, and other relationships held throughout life. Many successful academics fail to be successful administrators not because they do not understand the issue at hand but because they can not get along well with their coworkers; writing, verbal, and non-verbal communications, all of these prove the worth of a successful academic administrator. I have been very lucky as an administrator here in Uganda, Africa and many other places in the world including the United States because of my ability to recognize my weaknesses and strengths as I work others in life relationships. The purpose of this presentation to the workshop of those who came to listen to me is to understand my leadership ability and utilize my teachings back home. This was a group of about 200 people in attendance.

SKILLS OF A SUCCESSFUL ADMINISTRATOR

Three important skills are virtual necessary for one to be a successful administrator. They are:

I. Technical skills—It is the level an individual is trained in ether schools and colleges and seminar and workshops. The training one acquires in a school improves his/her competent to deal a a massive world wide population.

II. Human Relations skills—A major effort is recently made of recently for social scientists and psychologists to study the behavior of human beings both at home and at works. How we deal with each other. Highly intellectual scholars fail to work to go along with people. In the system of human relations is the proper understanding with human diversity and ethnic integration of our society and work place. We need to force to learn each other and understanding diversity. The supervisor evaluates employee depending on the environment and the experience of those you lead. Better to always use : "Swot" strengths, weakness , opportunity and threat. An administrator is measured also on how he manages the budget and goals of the organization. That war, a successful administrator depends on people to manage outside world.

Conceptual skills are derived upon, the historical way an administrator made decisions over major issues. In application for employment, the "Resume" tend to provide how a candidate for a job would have made decisions that determines his leadership experiences. Resume are usually an address to focus on the way a successful administrator has had promotions and ability to control organizations on behalf of the owners of the organizations (e.g. hospitals, banks, business stores, Universities, schools and etc. The smooth decision making of the past is a total correction in the " resume, which is a conceptual related skills the administrator has had in the past.

Anyway Poem: By Professor Edward Khiwa Philosophy for the Services & Respond to Challenges of life

People are unreasonable, illogical and self- centered, love them anyway!

If you do good , people will accuse you of selfish ulterior motives, do good anyway!

If you are successful, you will win false friends and true enemies; succeed anyway!

Honesty and friendliness makes you vulnerable. Be honest and friendly anyway!

People favor underdogs, but follow only top dogs. Fight for some underdogs anyway!

What you spend years building may be destroyed overnight. Build anyway!

People really need help, but may attack you if you help them. Help people anyway!

Give the world the best you have and you'll get kicked in the teeth. Give the world the best you've got anyway!

Professor Edward Khiwa

GLOSSARY

Kenya (pgs 48) .... a nation with uganda boarder; Kapala (pgs51) capital of uganda
Rumbling guns (pgs52) shooting at night Bule and Bweya (pgs 56) family of luyirika' s birth place. Queens (pgs 10) No queens in buganda;500 years (pg10 est. longivity of Buganda kingdom. Lelegacy of Arab trade (pgs 13) Hunting white ants (pgs17);Moment of silence (pgs 46);Words of wisdom (pg 44);African ethnic diversity (pgs 144); Diaspora (pgs 143); Godwin Kiwuwa (pgs 153 first son of the author); night dancer carrying his dead body victim (pgs 147); Kigeya -Mikaya Bayise, father of both sons:Erisa Salongo, Luyirika and Walungama Jonathan Musoke. (Kigeya Bayise the father of both was burried at Namakofu in the ground of Erisa Luyirika estate); Today, it is a collection home for all of Luyirika's family led by Dr. Joshua Kigeya who resides in both America and Uganda. The home of Jonathan Musoke Walungama at Namakofu is managed by Professor Edward Kiwuwa–Khiwa.
Luyirika (name of the father of the author and heritage of learned families of Baganda in Uganda).........pg 1.
Kabaka (King)
Kiwuwa (One of the names of the author of " What my father told me at three ") –- Pg1
Baganda (name of dominant kingdom in Uganda, and members of it, their identity is Baganda, and one is Muganda.
Inca and Aztec (Identity of former powerful kingdoms in S. America, (destroyed), decimated due to welcoming in foreign culture and foreigners in their kingdoms, without regulatory agencies and pre-selecting (pg 4)

Winston Churchhill......... former prime minister of England that saved the kingdom during WWII.... scared Hitler with words of enthusiasm "We will fight, but never surrender".......pg5.

Kikuyu...... One of the Kenyan citizen, dominant tribes in its leadership & Kenyata --- pioneer first President of Kenya— pg 6 French, English & Arabs. Former colonial legacy with lasting cultural influence in Uganda and Africa (Swahili language) pg6 Debate against civilian democratic style and Feudal system of governance.... pg 7

Effect of internet to culture and global civilization......... ......pg7

Sickle Cell diseases——— Mosquitoes and hereditary diseases (Immunity from it)pgs8

REFERENCES

(1) Seaway, Moses ; wars of 60's – Present, Ida Amin; A Novel: Abyssinian Chronicles, Amsterdam, Netherlands, Publishing, (November 13, 2001)
(2) McDonnell, J.H. Faith: Girls Soldier's Story of Hope for Northern Uganda's Children, Netherlands, Publishing 2001
(3) Kapuscinski, Ryzzard; The Shadow of the Sun, Maranatha Publishing press, kampala, Uganda (2005)
(4) Isegawa, Moses, "Snake pit", A novel, Idi Amin over Uganda and its people, Maranatha publishing, 2011
(5) Guide, Brandt : "Travel to Uganda, 7th ed. Jon Blanc, 2013
(6) Liyong, 1 Taban: "Uganda literacy desert"(1969) & Oscar Ransom (2013): The little of Mind" (Ranzo Publishing 2013)
(7) McDonnell, Faith, Akallo, Grace, Haselltine, (June1, 2007; Girl Soldier : A story of Hope for Northern Uganda's Children, Africa Press 2011
(8) Branch, Adam, Displacing Human Rights: war and interventions in Northern Uganda, Africa Press (2011)
(9) Mwaki Kagile, Godfrey, "The land and its people, Africa Press (2009)
(10) Scherz, China: having people, Having heart, Charity Sustainable Development, and problems of Dependence, in Central Uganda, Africa (2014)
(11) Simon Dunstaw & Peter Dennis: Israel's lightning Strike, The Raid on Entebbe 1976.(12)Kodesh, Neil: "beyond the Royal gaze, Clanship and public Healing in Buganda, Maaranatha Press, Kampala, Uganda (2000)

(13) Naipaul, Shiva, North of South: An African Penguin, Journey Classic, 20th century, Penguin 1977
(14) Patterson, John, Henry," The Man Eaters of Tsavo: And other East African Adventures, Penguin 2013
(15) Crothers, Tim, "The Queen of Katwe: One Girls' Triumphant Path to Becoming a Chess Champion, Penguin 2013
(16) Stevenson, Terry & Fanshawe, J. The Birds of east Africa: Kenya, Tanzania, Uganda, Rwanda and Burundi, Princeton field Guides, 2002
(17) The Baganda, reading Culture and literacy in Uganda, Children's' Reading Tent, penguin Publishers 2001

www.ingramcontent.com/pod-product-compliance
Ingram Content Group UK Ltd.
Pitfield, Milton Keynes, MK11 3LW, UK
UKHW022227230426
12048UKWH00016BA/1109